IN NAPOLEONIC DAYS

IN NAPOLEONIC DAYS

EXTRACTS FROM THE PRIVATE DIARY OF
AUGUSTA, DUCHESS OF SAXE-COBURG-SAALFELD,
QUEEN VICTORIA'S MATERNAL GRANDMOTHER

1806-1821

SELECTED AND TRANSLATED BY

H.R.H. THE PRINCESS BEATRICE

WITH A FOREWORD BY

JOHN VAN DER KISTE

A & F Reprints

First published by John Murray 1941
This edition first published by A & F 2020

Foreword © 2020 John Van der Kiste

A & F Publications
South Brent, Devon, England TQ10 9AS

Typeset 11pt Book Antiqua

ISBN 9798640866209

Cover illustrations: Augusta, Duchess of Saxe-Coburg-Saalfeld; View of
Coburg, c.1810

Printed by KDP

CONTENTS

FOREWORD

Shortly after the outbreak of the Second World War in September 1939, Princess Beatrice undertook to translate the diary of her great-grandmother, Augusta, Duchess of Saxe-Coburg-Saalfeld. The extracts covered the years 1806 to 1821, including the marriage of the Duchess's daughter Victoire to Edward, Duke of Kent, the father of Queen Victoria and fourth son of King George III.

At the time, Princess Beatrice was aged eighty-two. The youngest child of Queen Victoria, she was one of the three still alive. Of the others, Louise, Duchess of Argyll, died in December 1939 and Arthur, Duke of Connaught, in January 1942, both at the age of ninety-one. Married to Prince Henry of Battenberg in July 1885, she was widowed only ten and a half years later when he died of enteric fever, after having been sent home while serving with the army in Africa. They had four children, three sons and a daughter, the latter becoming Queen Ena of Spain, the long-suffering wife of King Alfonso XIII. Beatrice outlived two of their sons, Maurice, who was killed during the First World War in 1914, and Leopold, who had inherited the hereditary disease of haemophilia and failed to survive what should have been a routine medical operation in 1922.

For health reasons, she moved from Kensington Palace to Ravenswood, near Sharpthorpe in East Sussex, in 1939, and subsequently to another house in the same area, Brantridge Park, near Balcombe. Illness, particularly bronchial asthma, had greatly curtailed her activities. Yet for a long time she had considered working on the diaries, if only for her own amusement and enjoyment. Soon after she had started, it occurred to her that a book based on the diaries might appeal to readers, partly because of the family connection, and partly because there was a similarity between the days of the Napoleonic wars and the European conflict that had just begun.

Half a century earlier, John Murray had published her translation of Emil Kraus's *The Adventures of Count Georg Albert of Erbach*, which had been a modest success. More recently the same company had issued *The Letters of the Prince Consort*, an officially approved selection edited by Dr Kurt Jagow, and sent her a complimentary copy. Murray was therefore an obvious choice when it came to seeking a publisher, and the Princess's lady-in-waiting Minnie Cochrane approached the firm in October 1940. Murray replied to place on record his agreement in principle, but said he would need to see the manuscript first so that he could produce an estimate of the likely cost. After King George VI and Queen Mary had read the typescript, it was sent to him. He agreed to publish, and chose the title *In Napoleonic Days* with which the Princess immediately agreed.

Because of wartime shortages and restrictions, publication was slightly delayed. Fortunately the typescript needed only a minimum of little editorial work, and just one stage of proofs was required. It was published on 12 June 1941. Despite an error in the initial publicity material advertising the price as eighteen shillings instead of the correct price of seven shillings and sixpence, 230 advance copies had been sold to booksellers by the eve of sale. 1514 copies were printed, with seventy-seven being offered to members of the press, and sales of at least a thousand being necessary to cover expenses. This figure was not merely reached but surpassed within four months, with the last eighteen being sold by February 1943.

In a review in *The Spectator*, 20 June 1941, Vivien Bartley wrote:

It would be attractive to compare the Duchess Augusta with her granddaughter Victoria; even in the brevity of a review some traits may have suggested themselves to the reader. In a much-quoted passage, [Lytton] Strachey compared the young Princess's diary to a smooth, opaque pebble; this Journal, so ably edited by Princess Beatrice (who herself must have wonderful memories to tell), is more nearly a small, rounded mirror, candid and clear, where Napoleon's Europe smoulders in minute reflection.

It had thus proved a satisfying success for Princess Beatrice in the evening of her days. She died in October 1944, aged eighty-seven.

I bought a copy in a secondhand bookshop in January 1978 for the princely sum of fifty pence, admittedly without a dust jacket, slightly worn cloth binding and missing the front free endpaper. Some forty years later, I was astonished to find out how rare it was. A thorough search online revealed no copies for sale, only the information that one with a stained, incomplete jacket had recently changed hands at an Oxfam shop specialising in collectables, for £70. As a contribution to royal reminiscences of the Napoleonic period, as well as a very elusive work in its own right, I am pleased to be able to help make this widely available for the first time since its first appearance in an era when circumstances necessitated a very limited edition.

For details of the book's publishing history as given above, I am indebted to the account in Matthew Dennison's biography, *The Last Princess: The devoted life of Queen Victoria's youngest daughter* (Weidenfeld & Nicolson, 2007).

The text of this edition remains unaltered, apart from a few additional footnotes and occasional supplementary information in those that appeared in the original. For ease of reference, I have added brief notes on the family of the Duchess.

John Van der Kiste

INTRODUCTION

The King having kindly given me his permission to translate for publication some extracts from my Great-Grandmother's Diary, I hope that this small effort and venture of mine may be of some interest to the public, and ultimately benefit the funds of various War Charities.

My Great-Grandmother, the Duchess Augusta of Saxe-Coburg-Saalfeld, was the daughter of Prince Reuss-Ebersdorf. She was born in 1757 and in 1777 married Franz, Duke of Saxe-Coburg-Saalfeld, by whom she had several children, including Queen Victoria's mother, the Duchess of Kent (Victoire in this diary); Leopold, husband of Princess Charlotte of Wales and afterwards first King of the Belgians; Sophia, Countess Mensdorff-Pouilly; Antoinette, married to Duke Alexander of Württemberg; Juliana, Grand-Duchess Constantine of Russia; Ernest, afterwards reigning Duke of Saxe-Coburg-Gotha and father of the Prince Consort; and Ferdinand, who married Maria II da Gloria Queen of Portugal and became King of Portugal under the title of Ferdinand II. The Duchess died in 1831. Of her Frederic Shoberl wrote in 1840, "Gifted with a superior understanding and adorned with rare accomplishments, this princess united all the softness of her own sex with the firmness of the other. Undaunted by the storms of fate she never lost sight for a moment of her destination as a wife and mother."

Her original Diary is in the family archives in Windsor Castle and, so far, the extracts from it have only been printed in German for private circulation. The curious similarity between the days of the Napoleonic wars and our own times has led me to think that this Diary might appeal to some readers, interested in that period. The record is very simply told and contains many references to the Duchess's family and the part they played in her life, but these could not be easily eliminated without spoiling the impression given by her graphic descriptions of the time in which she lived, in the Germany of that day so different from present-day Germany.

.

THE FAMILY OF AUGUSTA, DUCHESS OF SAXE-COBURG-SAALFELD

Countess Augusta Reuss of Ebersdorf (1757-1831), daughter of Henry XXIV, Count Reuss and Countess Caroline of Erbach-Schönberg, m. 1777, Francis, Duke of Saxe-Coburg-Saalfeld (1750-1806), Duke 1800-6

They had ten children (one stillborn), with all but two of the other nine surviving to adulthood:

Sophie Frederica (1778-1835), m. 1804 Emanuel, Count von Mensdorff-Pouilly (1777-1852)

Antoinette (1779-1824), m. 1798 Duke Alexander of Württemberg (1771-1833)

Juliana (Julie) (1781-1860), m. 1796 Grand Duke Constantine Paulowitsch of Russia (1779-1831), brother of Tsar Alexander I, and took name Anna Feodorovna, div. 1820

Stillborn son (1782)

Ernest I, Duke of Saxe-Coburg Gotha (1784-1844), m. 1817 Louise of Saxe-Gotha-Altenburg (1800-31), div. 1826. Their younger son Albert married Queen Victoria of England and became Prince Consort

Ferdinand (1785-1851), m. 1815 Maria Antonia ('Tony') von Kohary (1797-1862). Their eldest son Ferdinand (1816-85) became King Ferdinand II of Portugal, while a grandson became Prince (later King, or Tsar) Ferdinand of Bulgaria

Victoire (1786-1861), m. (1) 1803 Emich Carl, Prince of Leiningen (1763-1814); (2) 1818 Edward, Duke of Kent (1767-1820). Their daughter became Queen Victoria of England

Marianne (1788-94) – *died in infancy*

Leopold (1790-1865), King of the Belgians 1831-65, m. (1) 1816 Charlotte of Wales (1796-1817), daughter of George, Prince of Wales, later King George IV of England; (2) 1830, Louise of Orléans (1812-50). Their children included Leopold II, King of the Belgians and Carlota, Empress of Mexico

Francis (1792-3) – *died in infancy*

ILLUSTRATIONS

Map of the major German states, 1820

1806

April 2nd. The moon shines cold and bright in a cloudless sky. The mild breath of Spring has given way to cold biting east winds. It seems as if nature had allied itself with humanity to destroy all thoughts of happiness. There are nothing but storms in the atmosphere and amongst men. Poor Germany, what will thy fate yet be, given over to the caprices of a despot, who recognises no law but his own will, who sees no limit to his own lust for power, and to whom all means are justifiable to gratify this passion.

Soon to be under the yoke of an arrogant, grasping people, what future can my poor devastated country expect, she who once in olden days defied the Roman Eagle! When the short shameful war broke out, I foresaw a dark future, but now that the war has ended so disastrously my heart is filled with a nameless dread. Slowly and heavily the storm is creeping over Saxony. I wonder I shall finish these entries and in what place I shall lay my weary head to rest, after life's storms have passed over me? How much to be envied are our ancestors, who were put to rest in their native soil, and closed their eyes peacefully and happily, confidently cherishing the hope that their descendants would inherit the land of their fathers and live there undisturbed! But soon there will no longer be left a German Prince, to come into his inheritance.

April 6th. I cannot help wondering at some people's light-heartedness, standing, as we are, on the brink of an abyss. With each day Germany's position becomes more critical. It would suffice for one word from this all-powerful Despot, and we should no longer exist. Amidst all this uncertainty as to our future, we have to continue quietly with our usual mode of life, even to the giving of balls and attendance at the theatre. But how could one stand such a position, if we did not make some attempt at cheerfulness!

August 15th. At last the terrible blow has fallen which wrecks the German Constitution! Francis II has laid down the German Imperial Crown. In spite of the flaws in the old régime it surely is better than what we are going to be given in its stead. The ancient national oak, with its mouldering trunk and weather-beaten branches in which Wotan's eagle has for 1000 years had its eyrie, cannot be expected to stem the present tide of events, but it still could have afforded shelter to many a traveller, and a quiet tiller of the soil might have made himself a peaceful abode under its shadow.

The German Princes, owing to weakness and self-seeking, have estranged themselves from their Country. The Rhine Alliance was the cause of its most grievous wound, and Francis's cowardly resignation of the crown worn by the Hapsburgs for so many centuries, now gives the poor country entirely over to the successful adventurer, who founds his greatness on destruction, and who, soon to be crowned with the diadem of Cæsar, will rapidly and completely enslave it. Shall we, North Germans, be engulfed in the stream or shall our existence survive for a time the Holy Roman Empire? Oh Father of mankind, Who weighest in the balance the destiny of States as well as that of individuals, without Whose will not a hair of our heads falls, Thou wilt surely save us when the need arises!

September 28th. A false rumour last night that a French Cavalry Brigade was approaching, caused great distress in the town and deprived us of sleep. It was "much ado about nothing." But I wonder if these disturbers of the peace may not some day unexpectedly descend upon us?

October 2nd (Saalfeld). I am still quite dazed by the rapidity of our departure and all the fatigue and worry of clearing up and packing. The last days at Coburg were detestable continual contradictory rumours, mistaken forecasts of possible events; varying advice as to whether the Duke should stay or go. Added to this the Duke's indecisions, and the deep-seated dread of an uncertain future. I shall never forget these anguished days. I came here very reluctantly and should have even preferred the unpleasantness of having the French quartered on us, to this troublesome and difficult "déménagement." But I have again, as so often before, had to sacrifice my own peace and wishes, to the will of others, and made the journey here in the worst of weathers, to find everything lacking. But now that the worst is over I am glad to have escaped from the everlasting discussions. Perhaps this hurried flight was not necessary? One of those mistaken impulses!

October 6th. I am feeling very sad and depressed to-day, haunted by nameless fears, and the rumour of the approach of the French! Reports of all kinds are crossing each other, according to one of these, the French had already entered the forest and taken Pätau. The Prussian Hussars are making their way to the forest. 500 Infantry are quartered in the town and neighbouring villages and guns have been placed on the heights. We therefore have only quitted Coburg to find ourselves actually in the war zone and we may perhaps also have to flee from Saalfeld. This feeling of uncertainty, of having no fixed abode and being continually engaged in flight, keeps me in a perpetual state of dreadful apprehension, for one cannot help realising that this is only the beginning of our period of trial.

October 7th. To-day Sophie,[1] her husband (Mensdorff) and their little son Hugo have arrived. Thank God that they got safely through the forest! The crucial moment is approaching even nearer, when Peace of War will be decided upon. Germany's fate still lies in the balance. In a few weeks, maybe, we shall be saved, or – crushed out of existence!

October 10th (at night). Merciful God, what terrible times we have lived through! The grim memories of these days of bloodshed will never leave me. Already at ½ p. 8 my niece sent for me. Her corner room overlooked on the one side Waldbergen, through which the road from Coburg passes. On the left, shots were falling at intervals, as well as in and around the little village of Garnsdorf, at the foot of the hills, where the Prussian Jägers were posted. The ground above the forest was also being occasionally shelled. Prussian Batteries were stationed in the fields near the high road to Rudolstadt, and on the road itself, Fusiliers.

[1] Sophie Frederica Louise, eldest daughter of the Duchess, b.1778, m. in 1804 to Emanuel, Count Mensdorff-Pouilly, d.1835.

Towards 8 o'clock Prince Louis Ferdinand[1] arrived on the scene, rapidly followed by Horse Artillery and 2 Saxon Infantry Regiments. In the distance their fine band could be heard, and lately our brave Saxon Hussars came by, at a quick trot.

Prince Louis Ferdinand accompanied by his A.D.C.s reviewed all the troops, his brave, débonnaire appearance creating a general sense of confidence.

One could see the enemy coming down the hills, and hear the tramping of the Infantry and the sound of bugles. The whole scene of bloodshed lay spread out before us. The fire of the Prussian Battery was incessant, but the French guns seldom came into action. Their Cavalry emerged from the forest and streamed along in a never-ending and terrifying procession. One could see from the windows the Prussian shots falling amongst them and the manner in which they closed up their ranks. It was a dull, misty morning, but the sun came out later and one could distinguish quite clearly loose horses running about, whose riders were either wounded or dead. For some time I had almost the impression of watching ordinary Manœuvres, until the sight of a mortally wounded Saxon Hussar being carried past made a cold shiver run down my back, each time I heard a shot. The cannon-balls whistled past quite close to the Schloss, and yet no one would come away from the window to which we were as if glued, in the midst of our fright. At every moment fresh French Infantry emerged from the forest, passing through Garnsdorf; the German Batteries thundering away ceaselessly and one could, in between, discern the crackling of the Saxon rifles. A terrible blood-curdling din was kept up by drums and bugles.

Our dinner was brought up to us, but who could eat at such a terrible moment, when human beings were bleeding to death from thousands of wounds? Now, the sun appearing out of the cloudless sky lit up the scene of horror. We could realise only too well the great strength of our opponents, and petrified with fear, we awaited the end of the tragedy. I cannot describe my feelings when the moment arrived of inevitable surrender to superior forces. It was a moment of unspeakable anguish. The combatants disappeared behind the hill near Willsdorf and the sounds of fighting died away. With our eyes staring at the empty fields, the scene of much carnage, and frozen

[1] Prince Louis Ferdinand of Prussia.

with fear, we awaited the return of the victor and I am still almost paralysed with the horror of seeing the red Hussars rush into the town shouting and firing, threatening to cut down the Guard at our doors; only Mensdorff's presence of mind saved us. Infantry came now from Graba, bringing with it all the horrors of an undisciplined rabble. Since 4 o'clock, they have been engaged in pillaging the unfortunate town.

October 11th. How much more quietly this day has ended. A feeling of security returned to us, poor terrified ones, with the arrival of Maréchal Augereau. There was no noise in the house to remind one of yesterday's hours of terror. May God reward him for the measure of peace that has returned to this house, of which we were sorely in need, after a dreadful night following on the horror of the day.

It may have been 4 o'clock yesterday afternoon, when Maréchal Lannes, accompanied by a huge Staff, entered the Schloss. Tired and shaken by all our agitating experiences, we were still standing together, discussing matters, when he rode up. The coarse insolence of his followers, the arrogance of the Maréchal and the noise caused by their arrival was like that produced by rough customers entering a common inn. This added to the hopeless discomfort of our position. The courtyard was soon filled with prisoners and wounded. Everything that could be found in the way of kitchen utensils was requisitioned. Nothing was good enough for them and they treated our servants with great roughness and insolence. Mensdorff, grief-stricken as he was by the death of his great friend Prince Louis, moved backwards and forwards looking after things. Officers came with demands which could not be complied with. If any of our little circle plucked up courage to take a look outside, they were terrified by the red glow in the dark sky caused by a village burning in the distance.

October 12th. Maréchal Lannes, with his numerous and noisy suite, left us yesterday. In the midst of the turmoil of departing and arriving officers, something drew me to the window to watch a warlike scene. A detachment of Infantry with its eagles, preceded by bearded sappers, marched into the courtyard carrying something on poles. Only when they dropped their burden on the ground did I recognise the body of Price Louis Ferdinand. Naked and only wrapped in a rough cloth, lay this great Prince, his fine head uncovered. No wound had disfigured his beautiful face. At the back of the head there were some slight contusions, but in the bared breast yawned a deep wound, which had put an end to his life.

As suddenly as they had come, the beaters left again, leaving the corpse of the grandson of a King abandoned on the ground, like some victim of a common murderous assault. I could hardly see for tears, when Mensdorff came rushing out to accompany his friend's body to the Royal Vault. "Faites vous gloire de render les derniers honneurs à un héros." These words of his addressed to Maréchal Lannes' Hussar officers rang out sharp and clear, and they dismounted and carried the precious burden in solemn procession to its last peaceful resting place. A moment before his departure, Maréchal Lannes and General Victor came to see us. Lannes was haughty and cold; he requisitioned more horses and I could have almost cried when I saw my beloved black ones bearing harnessed. General Victor did not utter a word. What a blessing were the few hours of peace before we had to pull ourselves together to face the disturbance caused by a fresh arrival of troops. A few hours before Maréchal Augereau's advent, an A.D.C. arrived, whose aspect gave us courage. The Maréchal's behaviour fulfilled my hopes; he came with a moderate-sized Staff, brought order into chaos, and gave us every protection.

In the evening. Early this morning Augereau left again, and it is now settled that we shall leave Saalfeld tomorrow at mid-day. I am heartily glad to be returning again to Coburg.

October 15th (Coburg). It is as if I awoke from a bad dream, to find myself after a fortnight again in the place I had had to quit so hurriedly! Sick at heart I left poor ravaged Saalfeld. Immediately behind the town, we had to pass the battlefield still strewn with the unburied bodies of Prussian and Saxon Hussars lying near their slaughtered horses. The road was crowded with all manner of French Transport. All the villages we passed had been completely sacked and the inconsolable inhabitants stood weeping in front of their devastated homes waiting hopelessly for fresh disaster to overtake them.

October 18th. A fearful battle is said to have taken place near Jena, the town having been completely sacked and burnt out. Oh God!

16

what has become of Ernest[1] during these days of carnage and destruction? His great height increases my anxiety for him.

October 20th. Good Mensdorff left us to-day. May God's blessing go with him!

October 25th. The news to-day has utterly crushed me. The Prussians have been beaten at every point, pushed back and entirely split up. Oh God! where can Ernest be? I have heard nothing of him since the fateful 10th. My anxiety is turning to despair.

October 29th. How despicable is the way in which Napoleon has taken his revenge on the poor old Duke of Brunswick,[2] who, dying of his wounds at Blankenburg, was informed that he would be considered a prisoner of war, if he remained there. A really great man would have spared the aged and distinguished enemy any further humiliation, but the vindictive Italian cannot refrain from kicking the fallen. The fate of this excellent man, whose youth and middle age were so brilliant, touches me profoundly. What has the power crazed conqueror in store for the family and country of his foe?

November 4th. After being plundered and humiliated, the Saxon Army is said to have obtained being considered as neutral; but under what conditions will this have been? Oh! My poor country!

November 7th. Napoleon has refused neutrality to Saxony, contrary to what had been said a few days ago.

With every step into the enemy's country, the conqueror raises his demands, and our ruin becomes more certain. His despotic plans become more and more ambitious. At first he sought in various ways to overcome Germany's distrust. Only with many plausible pretexts, finally to enslave her. Now the lucky conqueror will carry out with severity his plans, which might have been applied gradually and by more artful means. Germany's ancient Princely Houses must now bend their proud necks under his iron sceptre. They will fall, but in

[1] Ernest Antony Charles Louis, eldest son of the Duchess, b. 1784, serving in the Russian Army, d. 1844.
[2] Charles William Ferdinand, Duke of Brunswick, b. 1735, d.1806.

their hearts harbour a secret contempt for the arrogant and fortunate adventurer, who so unjustly exercises his power. He will make his insatiable relations Princes of the land. What then, will be our fate? That lies in God's hands. Whatever our lot may be, no human tyranny can deprive us of His care, and finally we shall be enlightened and realise that in His ways lies wisdom, much as our hearts may have rebelled against His decrees.

November 13th. Each day the news becomes sadder. The Hessians have been disarmed; although neutrality had been promised to the "Churfürst"[1] the unfortunate country is being treated as "pays conquis." Possibly what remains of the Prussian Armies may be already fighting against the superior foes on the Baltic. Prussia is succumbing without a chance of being saved. In the midst of all this distressing news — still none of Ernest and no possibility of bringing him back.

November 16th. Our unfortunate lot is now decided. The order was issued to-day that all revenues are to be sequestrated by the Emperor and no further monies paid out. I am positively petrified with fear. How will the poor Duke's health stand this blow?

November 23rd. How easily one is ungrateful to Providence when in great trouble. I am so filled with anxiety for Ernest, that I am not sufficiently thankful that the Duke's health is fairly good this autumn.

November 30th. At last a letter from Ernest. Thank God, he was safe and well on the 11th! How can the King [of Prussia] remain quietly in Graudetz whilst the Conqueror is robbing him of Province after Province, Poland being turned upside down and the whole of Germany being enslaved by the tyrant? Germany owes her downfall to her faulty constitution and Prussia owes hers to the deterioration of her monarchy. And yet she never had a better intentioned ruler than Frederick William! He, who always sees through the eyes of others and acts according to the will of others, becomes, as an ordi-

---

[1] William I, "Churfürst" or Elector of Hesse., b. 1743, d. 1821.

inary individual, the tool of deceivers and, as a monarch, the victim of powerful, scheming neighbours.

December 4th. For many years, this month has always been one full of trouble for me, and since the Duke's[1] illness, I cannot help starting It with some trepidation. This time too the month keeps up its reputation. Early this morning I was rendered very angry and quite ill by an abominable article in the Erlagen newspaper concerning the Duke. He did not read it himself, having been attacked by a sharp touch of fever, probably due to a chill, which has made me quite anxious, however I hope it will not be followed by any ill effects. Howe hard to have fresh worry on this score.

December 8th. The Duke's health causes me great anxiety, the fever has not abated and his nervous and restless condition increases it! This evening when he got up to have dinner, he seemed to me terribly exhausted and his poor face looked so drawn. I am so distressed and worried by his constantly expressed longing for Ernest. Oh! surely the poor Father will not pass away without the comfort of seeing his son again.

December 9th (early). With what dread in my heart I started this day! I was summoned to the Duke at 3 o'clock and found him in a very nervous condition with a high fever. He wanted to say good-bye to me, though the Doctors did not anticipate any immediate danger. He spoke in a louder and more hurried tone than usual. After 4 o'clock I went back to bed, and on my return at 7, found him in the same condition. He seemed to me to be very nearly in a coma, the pulse had slowed down and the Doctors appeared to be taking a grave view of the situation. Oh God! the dread of what may come quite kills me!

December 10th. All is over! The dear life is spent, which has caused me for 4 years so much anxiety. I feel quite stunned by the shock, for which I have to a certain extent been so long prepared, though I did not quite expect it at this moment. How deep is then pain for the loss of this dear companion, by whose side I have walked for nearly 50 years. I cannot collect my thoughts, but I must thank a merciful God

[1] Francis, Duke of Saxe-Coburg-Saalfeld, husband of the Duchess.

for having allowed the Angel of Death to release so gently the poor tormented body, and that He spared my dear one the death from dropsy, which he so dreaded.

December 15th. Coburg (Master of the Horse)[1] has returned from Prague this evening, but his journey proved useless as he could not get through to Ernest. Poor boy, what will he feel when he gets the news of his beloved Father's death. I wonder how soon he will get back to take over the Duchy which comes to him too early. Added to my heavy trouble comes the news of Ferdinand having to march with his Regiment in Hungary.

December 20th. I feel at the close of this day a peculiar sense of depression, such as I have never felt before. The French "Intendant," Vilain, arrived here to-day. I had to have him met as if he were a Prince.

December 21st. So our future has been decided upon! This afternoon Vilain appeared quite unexpectedly. The news of the ratification of our assent to the Rhine Alliance came as a complete surprise to me. This alliance of which I had such a horror, has now turned out to be for our good, and it saves us from immediate annihilation. How circumstances can change one's views! What finally will be decided about the future of poor devastated Germany, lies in God's hands. All praise to Him for our present position, which might have been very terrible had Napoleon given us away, as a conquered land.

December 28th. There are only a few days now to the end of the month, and to the year that has brought us so much anxiety and sorrow. No news of Ernest since he wrote 5 weeks ago! I start and end this day filled with the greatest concern for his safety.

December 31st. This year is just about to end and the next one will be the first for many years that I enter upon without my dear life-long companion at my side. Loneliness fills me with deep melancholy, but the arrival of good Mensdorff has shed a ray of sunshine on the departing year. As I saw with what joy Sophie welcomed her

[1] "Freiherr" Emil von Coburg, Councillor and Master of the Horse.

husband, I realised with a pang that I was now a widow, to whom no one is any longer all in all. My grown up children go their own way, and have their own interests which are different to mine. None but a married couple can entirely share each other's thoughts and pursuits. Nothing can replace this bond of love which only seemed to increase in strength with the passing years. Rest in peace, my beloved one; at the threshold of another year, I am remembering the many happy ones we spent together, never marred by a single word or action. I recall with gratitude all your goodness, your kindness, your gentleness and indulgence. We shall one day meet again in a better world!

1807

January 5th. My good Ferdinand[1] arrived from Vienna this afternoon unexpectedly. May God reward him for the haste with which he came to his mother.

January 8th. With every evening that closes my monotonous day, I think sadly to myself "Ernest is still not there!" His absence now, when each moment is critical, and his whole future is in jeopardy, drives me nearly crazy!

January 16th. At last news from Ernest, but not such as I would have wished. The dear thoughtless Boy seems to be going further north, instead of coming here, where his presence is so urgently needed. It is quite incomprehensible to me that he and his friends do not see the necessity for his quick return! Day and night I am tormented by the thought that I should not have let him go. The great distance between us, his position and the uncertainty of his return, are the greatest worries I have ever experienced. What a good thing that we cannot forsee the future. Had I known 4 months ago, what troubles were in store for me, I should never have been able to find the strength to face them.

January 18th (early). I have returned with melancholy feelings from Church where they held a Peace Celebration. May the present situation, in which we have been driven by dire necessity, prove not unhappy for the country and its Duke. Let us hope that the peace for which Saxony has paid such a heavy price will prove a lasting one. I prayed earnestly for God's blessing on my dear son on whom, the heavy responsibility of a Ruler has been all too soon thrust. What

[1] Ferdinand George Augustus, 2nd son of the Duchess, b. 1785, serving in the Austrian Army.

times we live in! I wonder if he is going to be as unlucky as his father was. God grant him wisdom and may his father's spirit guide him in his difficult task. I felt it deeply sitting alone in Church, in the same place where we always sat together.

January 25th. My presentiments have been only too fully justified. Ernest is lying ill at Koenigsberg with a nervous fever, and hundreds of miles lie between us. It is only after 4 or 5 weeks that I have been able to get news of the dear boy who was taken ill 6 weeks ago, and I wonder how it fares with him now? There are no words to express my anxiety, and I am utterly cast down.

January 28th. Merciful Father in Heaven, Thou hast not abandoned me and hast preserved my dear son's life. With tears of gratitude I thank Thee for having rescued him from the very doors of death, and that he is now on the road to recovery.

January 30th. Reluctantly I have come to the conclusion, that I shall have personally to defend my poor Ernest's cause with the Emperor Napoleon, and appeal to him for protection and help. The happiness of my children demands this sacrifice from me, which I make willingly. Only the pain of having to part with Ferdinand, sooner than I expected, now troubles me.

February 1st. I start this month with much apprehension, for during it such weighty decisions will be taken. To-morrow I shall start on my difficult mission. Only my love for Ernest could make this sacrifice possible for me. God protect me on my cold hazardous journey, and give His blessing to this undertaking of a troubled mother! Oh God, grant Thy help to a sorely afflicted family!

February 7th (Berlin). I arrived here yesterday evening, dead tired.

February 8th. Yesterday the Governor General Clarke and General Hulin. Commandant of Berlin, with a host of A.D.C.s came to me. Clarke is a big man, of distinguished appearance, and the look of an Englishman. He was very affable and civil, possessing the easy pleasant manner of the late French Count. Hulin's great big strong and very ordinary presence, reminded one of the days of the revolution. He was a Grenadier of the Garde Française, and the first to storm the Bastille. Gen. Clarke told me that the Emperor was not in Warsaw at present. Whatever is to become of me, and where shall I have to seek for the Emperor?

February 10th. One day after another goes by, without anything being decided as my unlucky journey. The Emperor is with his army — he may perhaps come to Warsaw – the roads are very unsafe — more than this I cannot find out. Obviously various movements of troops are going on, but if they do not result in a French victory, we shall be kept waiting for news for some time; and I, poor unfortunate, can meanwhile be of no use and am wasting my time and my money. It is a desperate position to be in.

February 14th. At last my movements are decided upon and I am leaving for Dresden in a couple of days, in order to ask the King of Saxony to use his influence on Ernest's behalf. I cannot go to Warsaw as things are at present and it would be useless to undertake the difficult journey, if I am not certain of finding Napoleon there. Besides, the constant fighting might easily make it dangerous.

February 19th (Dresden). Yesterday I spent a weary day travelling. We left Torgau at half-past seven in the morning. The flooded condition of the Elbe obliged us to take a roundabout way. Up to Strehlen the country was lovely, the Elbe was rushing through the flooded valley, every meadow was a lake full of islands, and the sun, shining through the leafless trees, lit up the scene. The fine, mild, springlike weather turned to rain in the evening, which never ceased from Minden onwards till we reached Dresden, which we did only at 11 o'clock at night, thoroughly tired out.

February 20th. Yesterday morning the Minister Count Bose and the sly old Count Marcolini came to see me, and were full of good advice and high hopes for the future adjustment of our troubles, but I only expect real help from God. To remain hopeful, when one has been so often disappointed, is very difficult. After the cheerfulness of the fine town of Berlin, Dresden strikes me as very dreary, rather like an old lady, tastelessly arrayed in heavy, unsuitable garments, defying modern times, whereas Berlin resembles an elegant young bride whom the war has hardly touched. This afternoon I have been bidden to the palace.

February 21st. It is impossible to have been more cordially or kindly received, than I was yesterday at the Palace. The King (Frederick Augustus),[1] who wears his thorny crown with the feelings of a slave in chains, appeared to me more talkative and sympathetic than usual. Misfortunes which he has never before experienced, have awakened his perceptions and made him take some interest in our troubles. The whole family overwhelmed me with friendliness, which in these dark days was very welcome.

The same evening. I visited the Picture Gallery to see the Masterpieces once more, before the possible removal of the best of them by Napoleon.

February 22nd. To-morrow I leave Dresden with no regret, for never has it seemed to me so depressing and tedious. I took leave at the Palace this afternoon, carrying away with me a warm feeling of gratitude for the most kind way in which the King and his family have received us. At Princess Anton's[2] I saw Prince Max's[3] children, nice, pretty little creatures, but who I am afraid are going to be handicapped by being brought up in the stiff, narrow formality of a bygone generation. This will not fit them for present-day conditions.

February 25th (Prague). It is not often that a wish such as mine to visit Julie[4] in Prague is so unexpectedly granted. The dear creature came part of the way to meet me. We were both delighted to see one another and I then drove with her into the ancient Royal city through endless tortuous streets till we came to her cheerful quarters on the Promenade in the new part of the town.

February 27th. To-day I had the great pleasure of receiving a few shaky lines from Ernest, the first he has attempted to write since his illness. May God be praised for having saved him on the very edge of the grave. On the 8th he could still hardly walk alone across the

[1] Frederick Augustus, King of Saxony, 1806-27 (Elector 1763-1806).
[2] Princess Marie Thérèse, daughter of the Emperor Leopold II, m. 1787 to Anton, Prince of Saxony, later, King.
[3] Maximilian, Prince of Savoy, brother of the King.
[4] Juliana Henrietta Ulrica, 3rd daughter of the Duchess, b. 1781, m. 1796 to Constantine Paulowitsch, Grand Duke of Russia.

room. I feel thoroughly happy and comfortable in Julie's charming home. I spent a pleasant peaceful morning in her dear company, which I had not enjoyed for a long time.

February 28th. As we returned in the evening from the Theatre, who should we find waiting for us on the stairs but Ferdinand! When I left Coburg I little thought I should see him so soon again, and it was a delightful surprise.

March 8th. With a heavy heart I have come to this last happy day in Prague. It is ages since I spent such happy carefree hours, which have flown like a dream. The peace and order which reigned in my dear Julie's house were most soothing to me. For the last 6 months I have not experienced such a tranquil time and it was such a blessing not to be forced to listen to unpleasant news. Ferdinand accompanied me a certain distance on his way to his Hungarian Garrison.

March 10th (Carlsbad). On first waking I had the pleasure of receiving a letter from Ernest, which Julie had sent on to me. Thank God! he has completely recovered and is, I hope, by now making his way home.

March 13th (Coburg). With a grateful heart, I am back here again. I have accompanied the journey I had undertaken so unwillingly, and with such misgivings and have done so without any mishap. If only I could have achieved the object, for which I set out!

March 17th. I am inundated with unpleasant news, nothing but complaints and tales of woe. The French Intendant Dumolard behaves very decently; but that does not alleviate the burden laid upon the people. The hope of any future prosperity is ruthlessly crushed.

March 18th. I cannot get accustomed to my loneliness, and I am feeling it more than ever to-day when Sophie and her sweet child have left the old home, to accompany her husband to Bohemia. I let her go most unwillingly, but I would not for the world spoil her pleasure at returning to her husband, after the sacrifice she has made in remaining so long with me. Leopold[1] and I are now the only inmates of the old "Schloss," and I would give anything, as I have

26

to remain here, to take a little house in the town, where there would be no memories or empty rooms.

[1] Leopold George Christian Frederick, b. 1790, youngest son of the Duchess. King of the Belgians, 1831-65.

March 25th. I have for once spent a cheerful evening, which is a rare thing. I went with Leopold and Malchen (my lady) to Ketschendorf.[1] After a very bright afternoon, there was a splendid crimson sunset, which lit up the whole country. Such a feeling of peaceful repose came over me, in the quiet homely little house, where one seemed to escape from the oppressive and lonely atmosphere of the "Schloss." We 3 sat down to a simple little tea, after which Leopold read aloud and the evening passed only too quickly.

March 26th. In this lovely weather Dumolard and Parigot also came to Ketschendorf. I had so dreaded their enforced company, but now I am ready to put up with this inconvenience as it is the only way in which I can show these gentlemen my gratitude for their pleasant behaviour. I feel that in making this sacrifice of my privacy, I may perhaps gain a little influence over them. Dumolard is good natured and obliging and he seems to realise the unmerited harshness of my plight and does all in his power to alleviate it. Proud and conceited as are most young Frenchmen, he is very susceptible to any little courtesy shown to him. Parigot is an excellent creature and full of good intentions to spare and be of service to us, but he is moody, indolent and easily offended. Entertaining these Gentlemen is hard work and needs much tact.

April 9th. Victoire[2] arrived this afternoon with her beautiful boy, who is full of life. It is very dear of her coming to me now, when I can offer her so little entertainment. The old paternal home is empty and lifeless; of all her brothers and sisters, only Leopold is here, and her dear father is for ever at rest. Mercifully sorrow does not weight long

[1] Ketschendorf, a village not far from Coburg, where the Duchess had a small country home.
[2] Marie Louise Victoria, 4th daughter of the Duchess, 1786-1861, m. 1803 to Charles Emich, Prince of Leiningen (d.1814), and afterwards to the Duke of Kent. Mother of Queen Victoria.

on young people, but at my age the wounds dealt to body and soul, are deep.

April 24th. To-day it is already a fortnight since Victoire came here, and brought a little life and brightness into our family circle, but alas! Time is flying. I have just returned rather tired, from a heavenly evening spent at Ketschendorf. The mild breath of spring revives the whole of nature, and it also raises the spirits of depressed mortals. Uncle Josias[1] and the French gentlemen joined us at tea and went back with us into the town. I continue to be very thankful that, although the sight of the latter gives me a pang, their friendliness and simplicity go a long way to reconcile me to their presence.

May 4th. We have spent the whole of this lovely May day at Ketschendorf. Victoire, Leopold and I sat watching several hundreds of Bavarians passing through, on their way to the "Grande Armée" who in no wise cover Napoleon's laurels.

May 7th. Early this morning the French Divisional General Bondet arrived, followed this afternoon by 2 thoroughly exhausted Regiments of Infantry. This Division has marched in 21 days from Venice. The General lunched with us. If his character is as gentle as his voice, then he is not likely to add to the oppression of the unhappy countries he is going to. He is a native of Guadaloupe and took part in the dreadful negro rising in San Domingo.

May 8th. French Infantry, about 1800 strong marched through the town to-day, making a halt in the market place, where they breakfasted and had a rest. The French are indeed a singular race, so light-hearted, and yet having wonderful powers of endurance. They made the long march from Italy over the Tyrolese snowy mountain passes, without taking one day's rest, which the Germans, on the other hand, would have insisted on, and ploughed through as if it were nothing unusual! What a pity that this nation, after all the horrors of anarchy, should have fallen into the hands of a heartless despot, who has known how to work upon their vanity and infuse into them his spirit of brigandage, and turn a happy-go-lucky people

---

[1] Frederick Josias, Prince of Saxe-Coburg-Saalfeld, 1737-1815.

into such scourges of humanity. One Division which came in the afternoon, has remained in the town.

May 14th. Since the 11th I have been expecting Ernest and now 4 days have passed by, and he is not yet here! I cannot understand the reason for this delay, and it is worrying me. Dumolard's doubts as to Ernest's coming is not the least of my worries. The French who are constantly deceiving us, do not easily believe in any sort of rectitude.

May 18th (Erkersreuth). Distracted at Ernest's inexplicable non arrival I took to my bed 2 days ago, and to-day I am sleeping under one roof with him! Thank God! he has completely recovered, only a certain lassitude in his movements is noticeable. I cannot describe the joy at having this longed for child with me again. God who so mercifully preserved him from death will surely dispel the dark clouds that hang over his future: I was hardly awake yesterday morning, when a letter was brought to me from Ernest begging me to meet him at Erkersreuth, and one from Kruschmann asking me to bring Dumolard with me. I did not at all relish coming here and would have far preferred to welcome Ernest at Coburg, aside his people's joyous acclamations.

May 22nd (Baireuth). I left Erkersreuth at mid-day to-day and should have much liked to spend a few more days with Ernest in that peaceful, quiet little place. It is a dreadful thought that he is prevented by that unjust tyrant from returning to his own rightful possessions.

May 25th (Coburg). My growing hope that Ernest after our many trials might see better days has been cruelly disappointed by Dumolard receiving a very curt letter from Daru, saying: "la présence du Prince ne change rien à vos fonctions." The poor dear boy has therefore sacrificed his pride all for nothing. It is set down clearly in Daru's letter that Ernest must proceed to Headquarters, there to receive from the Despot himself the final decision. Surely now that things are becoming stabilized, a fair minded monarch would terminate this sequestration of Ernest's possessions, which, if it drags on much longer, will certainly reduce us to penury.

May 30th. At last my ardent wish has been fulfilled. Ernest is here, but only to put in an appearance. Still the fact remains, that he has set foot again in his own country and it seems to me as if the charm were broken, which, since his departure, has brought on us poor creatures such a load of misfortune and trouble. Ernest, Leiningen and Leopold, have arrived this afternoon from Ebersdorf. Ernest wishes to spend the few days he is allowed to be here at Ketschendorf.

May 31st. All is quiet again here, after a mixture of pleasant and unpleasant experiences and I long for a little rest. Ernest has to retire early as he still gets very tired of an evening. We lunch and dine together, and this afternoon we had a little concert. I watched with an aching heart the pleasure of the good people of Coburg at seeing their Prince once more, many being touched almost to tears, and Ernest's scarcely concealed disgust at his humiliating position. He behaves so well and with such dignity and calm!

June 2nd. Ernest returned again to Eger this afternoon where he will spend the time till he has had his lands restored to him, and will take a cure there. I cannot blame him for wishing to escape from the oppression caused by the French administration of his dominions, but I much regret his departure.

July 8th. I am so out of sorts and deeply hurt that I can hardly control my thoughts. The two Emperors and the King of Prussia, have been conferring together at Tilsit. Alexander has obtained from Napoleon the return of Mecklenburg and the latter has agreed to this, but no one has given my poor Ernest a thought. He owes his present distressful position entirely to having adhered loyally to Prussia and no one has put in a word for him, when it would have cost them, nothing to get his property restored to him. This neglect on their part hurts me very deeply.

July 9th. Leopold has returned from Eger to-day. Ernest is still at Carlsbad and I am so afraid he may be losing valuable time just at this moment when his fate is to be decided upon. With youthful trustfulness he is hoping for help from his friends. But it is he himself who must take the matter into his own hands and every moment that is wasted may be irremediable.

July 16th. Deep in thought, I walked quite late, up and down in my garden, the moon shining faintly through the clouds. It was a very warm, calm night and one could hear across the meadows the plaintive sounds of the peasants singing songs. All of a sudden a footman appeared before me bringing a letter from Ernest. How thankful I am that he says he will not have to undertake the long and difficult journey to Tilsit. Napoleon is in Dresden, and Ernest is therefore hurrying to meet him there. He may not have to wait for many weeks, on the contrary, we may hope to see him quitter shortly once more in possession of his inheritance.

July 21st. Thanks be to Thee O God! who hast so mercifully protected us and not allowed us to sink under the weight of out misfortunes, to whom I also attribute the joy caused by the arrival of a "Courier" whom Ernest had sent from Dresden to acquaint both me and the whole of Coburg that the French authorities had received the order to hand over the Duchy to its rightful owner. It seems as if Ernest's troubles were clearing up and happier days were in store for him. Owing to Russia's kindly intervention he has been lifted out of the mire and the severe judge is turning into a magnanimous monarch!

July 28th (early). In another few hours Ernest will be returning to take up the reins of government. Everyone is on tip toe with excitement and dreams of giving him, whom they have been awaiting for so long, a great reception. I am so excited that I can neither sit still, read, or write. My heart is full of joy, but also of melancholy when I think that his beloved Father is no longer here to welcome him.

July 31st. Victoire, her husband, and adorable little boy went away this morning. How I shall miss them at every turn.

August 3rd. The French "Intendant" Dumolard left us this afternoon. Remembering my feelings of dismay and apprehension at his advent it does seem strange that now, I have taken a positively touching farewell, probably for ever, of this man whose attachment was almost filial, and who during the 7 months of his stay, never lost an opportunity of rendering service. He was always trying to make us forget the irksomeness of his presence in our midst. My best wishes accompany this really good young man, who performs his duties in so kindly a fashion and with a total absence of self-interest; this is a compliment which probably very few men in his position have deserved. His weaknesses, such as pride and conceit, are typical of his nation, whereas his virtues spring from his good heart.

September 11th. Herr von Dunkelmann arrived to-day from Paris. Ernest will have to go there, however much it costs him. I wonder if it is likely to help him in any way; not that I hope for great things from it! His presence in Paris is desired, and such a desire is tantamount to a command, which no German Prince dare disregard. Ernest wishes to take Leopold with him, and I have agreed to this, though with secret misgivings. He is so very young, but of course he would have to go out into the world, in order to complete his education, and this journey will help towards that end. I expect Julie in a few days and it is such a pity that she should see her brothers for such a short time, and then be left to share my loneliness.

September 20th. The news of Ernest's arrival in Paris is in the papers, but I have not heard a word from either him or Leopold. What will he feel to-day if he has to take part at Fontainebleau in the anniversary celebrations of the Battle of Auerstadt. It would be too awful for him should he have to participate in the triumph of his oppressor!

October 15th. To-day, I have received the first letters from my sons in Paris. Only after Ernest's visit to Fontainebleau shall we know if this costly journey has been any use.

October 24th. Yesterday I had some more news of Ernest. He has been presented to the Emperor who received him with courtesy and friendliness, and invited him to luncheon. Afterwards the mighty Ruler talked for two hours with the shy, inexperienced young man. But Napoleon never does anything without an ulterior motive and I wonder what can have caused him to single out my son for such an unexpectedly cordial reception. It fills me with uneasiness as to whether it will lead to any good and useful results.

November 11th. I am thoroughly overwhelmed between gladness and dread, and have hardly any strength to write. Ferdinand has been at death's door. To-day I received a letter, with his seal, but written in a strange hand, and when I opened it I saw that the signature was that of a physician. Inside was a slip of paper with Ferdinand's own writing on it and I jumped to the conclusion that it might be his last words of leave taking, but, thank God, his healthy constitution helped him to withstand and pull through the epidemic of fever, which was complicated by intestinal inflammation. He was taken ill on the 23rd of September in a miserable little Hungarian village, without any help, and without being able to obtain the most essential necessities and comforts. For the second time God has been merciful in sparing the life of another dear child. My heart is filled with gratitude for the preservation of this dear splendid boy!

November 16th. I get no letters, either from Paris or from Ferdinand and I am beginning to feel quite anxious.

November 21st. Ferdinand turned up to-day, white as a sheet and very shaky on his legs, but to my joy at having him safe back is added the fear that he may have undertaken the journey too soon. He is still very exhausted from his dangerous illness and there is no doubt that he is thoroughly tired out by the long journey.

December 24th. Thank God! that this day of sad memories is over! This used to be such a happy evening and now I look round with eyes dimmed with tears at the loneliness surrounding me and at the vacant place never to be refilled. My thoughts turn entirely to the past, and to the beloved one who used to delight in making me and the children happy on this Christmas Eve.

December 31st. This troubled year, the hardest in my life, which I entered upon with such anguish, is now drawing to its close. With deep gratitude, I thank God for having helped me through the bitter anxious hours, caused by the pressure of Napoleon's heavy mailed fist. How I thank Him for sparing the lives of my two sons, and preserving Antoinette[1] and Victoire during the dangers of their confinements. He will also surely help me to start the next year with courage and confidence.

[1] Antoinette Ernestine Amelia, 2nd daughter of the Duchess, b. 1779, m. 1798 to Alexander Frederick Charles, Duke of Württemberg.

1808

January 1st (Amorbach). After starting the last 2 years with tears, I close this first day of the new year, amidst the cheerfulness of a ball. The year started with a most lovely day, and an almost spring-like sun which we thoroughly enjoyed and there was a feeling of cheerfulness in the air. The dance was a very pretty one, and when we entered the ballroom, which was decorated with orange trees, the Grand Duchess was received by members of society in Russian peasant costumes, who sang Russian folk songs. It was a charming scene enhanced by little Charles who appeared as a Cossack with a bow and arrow, looking quite like a little Cupid, whose weapons he carried.

January 3rd. I am leaving this place to-morrow with great regret, having spent a most pleasant and peaceful 10 weeks here. I carry away with me the impression of a happy family life, which Victoire has known how to create around her. May such happiness be lasting!

January 11th (Coburg). Every step I take in the empty "Schloss" is dogged by memories of the past winter. It is more than a year now that I have had to live in this atmosphere of loneliness, Ernest has spent only a few weeks in his home, since the death of his Father, and it will soon be six months that he has not been here. Oh! if only this long and costly stay in Paris would lead to something good!

January 23rd. Thank goodness Ernest has at last taken the very necessary decision to be master in his own Duchy and free himself from the bullying domination of his Minister.

February 12th. Yesterday Sophie, her husband and little Hugo arrived quite unexpectedly, and I am delighted to have the dear people once more with me.

March 5th. I have had a letter from Ernest, which as usual, only throws out hopes, and says nothing definite as to the outcome of his journey or about his return home, and he has now been six whole months in Paris. I am really getting quite desperate!

March 16th. I have just been reading with horror and alarm a letter from Fraülein von Bussi, from Riga, telling me that Antoinette has been gravely ill with a nervous fever. Thank God! she was out of danger when the letter was written and I hope by now she is well on the road to recovery. It is dreadful to think that 4 weeks should have elapsed before the news reached me!

March 22nd. Ernest has sent Leopold on ahead, and I have been expecting him for the last three evenings. Certainly my patience is being put to the test!

March 23rd. Early this morning, Leopold at last arrived. He is astonishingly grown in these six months and has gained much in pose and appearance. I am so glad to have him here again, for he is really too young to be plunged into such a vortex of gaiety, without it becoming too attractive to him. The dissipations in the "grand monde" are like strong drink, they become a necessity, even if no pleasure is any longer found in them, and youths with impressionable and unspoilt natures, easily get demoralised.

April 21st. Thank God! Ernest arrived this afternoon, hale and hearty and still the same dear fellow.

May 8th (Ketschendorf). For the first time since last year, I have spent the night in this dear peaceful little retreat, but I could only enjoy part of the day, as already at 6 o'clock this morning, the Hereditary Prince of Mecklenburg Schwerin, appeared, on his way back from Paris, and a great part of the lovely spring day was wasted in tiresome formalities.

June 27th (Ketschendorf). Quite suddenly Hardenbrock burst in upon us this afternoon. God grant that his stay, of 8 months in St. Petersburg may have been of some use! The general delight of the whole family at the sight of this good, excellent man, must have proved to him that we value him as much as he deserves. I know few men possessing a stronger or more trustworthy character than he, gifted at the same time with the easy, pleasant manner of a man of the world. Never shall I forget his almost brotherly devotion to Ernest during his long dangerous illness. Antoinette was able to leave Riga on the 10th and Hardenbrock left her at Koenigsberg and travelled on ahead. What a joy it is to think that after such a long time I shall soon see the dear child again.

June 28th. My heart is heavy tonight and full of foreboding, so that I find it difficult to sit down and write. Ernest is expected to go to St. Petersburg in order to thank the Emperor for his intercession on his behalf and to crave his further protection, perhaps also he may find a wife amongst the Emperor's family. This possibility which ought to cause me great pleasure, fills me instead with some misgivings. Julie's fate keeps returning to my mind and never has she appeared to me more hurt, injured and neglected, than at the present moment and I cannot prevent my tears from falling at the thought of her. Her journey to Switzerland, which at the present moment I so much deprecate, oh! and many other things, that I cannot mention or write about, weigh heavily on my heart. We mothers have to experience much trouble as well as joy through our love for our children.

June 29th. The Hereditary Prince of Mecklenburg Schwerin has spent to-day with us. He is very pleasing and gentlemanlike and has a very nice face. He is quite a man of the world tinged with a slight romantic strain. He is the brother of the charming Queen of Prussia.

July 5th. Antoinette has at last arrived with her children. I cannot describe the joy it is, after 7 years to be able to embrace my beloved child again. It is a joy which only as mother would understand. Mariechen,[1] who was formerly such a droll little child, has grown up into a fine slender girl looking more like 11 than 9 years old, with an attractive clever face, though not exactly pretty. Her brothers are quite giants with nice looking fresh faces. Dear Antoinette has remained just the same, only grown a little stouter, than she left us last. She hardly recognised Victoire and Leopold after all this time.

July 7th (Ketschendorf). Early this morning Julie left, to spend the rest of the summer and autumn in Switzerland, Antoinette and Ernest accompanying her as far as Siman. In the afternoon we had a concert here and in the lovely summer's evening, we had a cheerful little supper.

July 13th. This afternoon Victoire left for Eger, where she is to take the waters. How soon this happy family gathering has dispersed, and I am left alone again! I find it difficult to accustom myself to these ever recurring partings and find it particularly hard that Ernest should again be leaving me and I wonder if this journey to St. Petersburg will be of any advantage to him. Will it, like the Paris journey, only result in waste of time and money, leaving him the poorer in purse and hopes? In my opinion, it would be far better if Ernest were to remain quietly here, instead of going to seek equivocal protection and doubtful happiness. But my feelings cannot decide this matter, and he is forced, however regretfully, to undertake the journey. May God protect and guide him.

August 4th. Ernest started on his journey to St. Petersburg to-day, accompanied by Hardenbrock and Szinborsky. The consequences of this journey may be very important, for they may lead to his future happiness or the reverse. I dare not express any wish and leave it to Thee, oh God! to decide my son's fate. I am full of sadness and anxiety.

August 7th (Baireuth). I unwisely left Coburg this afternoon at the hottest hour of the day. At 8 o'clock we got to Culmbach, where we stayed about an hour. French Cuirassiers are stationed there and their trumpeters, who are exceptionally good, were playing in the market place. Our drive on to Baireuth in the lovely warm summer night, lit up by brilliant moonshine, was very pleasant. It just struck 12 as we drove through the quiet streets here.

August 9th (early. Eger). The whole of yesterday was painfully hot, and everywhere we had to wait for horses, as they were all being used for the harvest, and we only got here at 9. Leopold went at once to bed, and I drove with Amalie into Franzensbad. As we entered the dining-room Victoire hurriedly got up from the supper table,

[1] Marie, Princess of Württemberg, m. in 1832 to Ernest, Duke of Saxe-Coburg-Gotha.

delighted but highly surprised at seeing us, and after having some supper, I made my way back to the town, as quickly as possible.

August 14th. Mensdorff came this morning to fetch Sophie. I have been very pleased to see him again. Alas, war may at any moment separate him from wife and child. The future fills me with a vague dread. The happy days spent together have flown only too quickly. What a pity that sometimes one cannot slow down the wheels of time in order to hold on a little longer to the few happy days one has in this short life. To-morrow Antoinette and I go to Töplitz, whither her children have preceded us to-day. Sophie, her husband, and Ferdinand are going to Franzensbad. The rumours of war that are being put about make me uneasy at parting from Ferdinand. It would be dreadful if he had to join his Regiment, without my being able to see him again!

August 23rd (Töplitz). We were just thinking of leaving the saloon at 10 to curtail the boredom of the slowly passing hours, when Ferdinand came in. His arrival cast quite a bright light on the stiff gathering, and a cheerful little supper ended the evening pleasantly.

August 24th. With each day the company grows smaller and becomes duller. The weather is splendid and the surrounding country is amongst the prettiest I know, but all the same an air of boredom seems to pervade the whole place. The mornings are occupied in taking the waters, the afternoons are spoilt by visits, and in the evening the guests reassemble far too early. I notice that the tone here amongst the visitors has greatly changed. There seems to be a certain constraint and lack of spontaneity and I am afraid we do not quite fit into the atmosphere. The young ladies are not attracted by us and we certainly are not attracted to them.

August 27th. Ferdinand's friends are rejoining their Regiment to-day, and in another 2 days he will also have to go. The scenery is so picturesque and the weather so fine, that I could do without company, but so Antoinette, accustomed to a more worldly life, society has become a necessity.

September 4th. Our days go by monotonously. The number of visitors keeps dwindling, so instead of sitting in the gloomy saloon, we drink tea at home, and in a smaller room the company seems more cheerful and friendly.

September 12th. Leopold, who had been to Gabel to see Ferdinand, returned this evening in good spirits.

September 14th (Franzensbad). After 2 days' weary travelling we got here this evening. Antoinette has got comfortable and pleasant lodgings, which rather compensate for the dullness of the place. Count Starenberg has made me rather nervous, by telling me that I might to-morrow, on the way to Baireuth, fall in with the French troops on the march, which would be almost as bad as meeting Red Indians. I would gladly remain here longer, but the horses are already ordered and I must therefore go.

September 17th (Coburg). The whole morning, yesterday, I was worrying about the possibility of meeting the French. At each stopping-place there were contradictory rumours, the only point on which they agreed was that the "Corps d'Armée", who had passed through, were thoroughly undisciplined and behaved like a band of robbers. Near Gerfräss our carriage broke down and we were obliged to have it repaired there. In a meadow near by, some baggage waggons, guarded by a few Infantry men, were drawn up, but that was the only thing we saw of the military. We got to Baireuth rather late, and to-day, at 7 o'clock, over bad roads, but in heavenly weather, we arrived here.

September 21st. Since Napoleon, like an evil genius, has been poisoning all the beautiful autumn days with horrors of war, one can no longer thoroughly enjoy them.
The persistent rumour that he will come to Erfurt in the next few days, much alarms me. What evil will that demon not be brewing again? I tremble at the thought. What if his plans were to bring him here? That would be too dreadful! The most fantastic rumours about his journey are spread about, and according to them, the Emperor of Russia would also be coming to Erfurt.

September 25th. Leopold went off early this morning to Erfurt, where it seems Napoleon and Alexander are really going to meet. I can only pray as one would before a bad storm; "lord, have mercy upon us!" Will this meeting decide the fate of the nations, or is it a theatrical gesture of this mighty demagogue, to conceal his bad position in Spain? How will one ever know? But this uncertainty haunts me.

September 29th. Antoinette returned from Franzensbad at mid-day, thoroughly tired out after a most unpleasant journey, and was greeted here by heavy rain. The children followed in the afternoon and the whole party are now housed in the Wangenheim house, which is none too big, and tired as they were, it was difficult to get them settled in.

October 1st. Early in the morning and in dreadful weather, Antoinette left for Erfurt with Prince Hohenlohe, who had been sent by her husband with despatches. Fräulein Buysy also accompanied her. May God give His blessing to their mission to the mighty monarch. All my thoughts are with them and I dread what this grasping autocrat's plans for us may be. It worries me so much that I can think of nothing else.

October 3rd. Incredible news comes from the small place on which the eyes of Europe and so many interests are warring against each other. Another week and then things will be made plain. Ernest's fate is now being cast. Oh! merciful Father, who has never forsaken our family, grant that it may prove a lucky one.

October 9th. A letter Antoinette has written to me from Weimar has much upset me, she tells me that the Grand Duke[1] (Julie's husband) has constantly been asking after me and my brother,[2] adding that I ought to have waited personally on the Russian Emperor, and now it is too late. I have sent Coburg to Erfurt to try to find out something as to the outcome of this obscure business.

October 10th. I am determined to go off to Saalfeld to-morrow, in order to meet the despatch rider Coburg is sending me. I do so, God knows, unwillingly and probably uselessly.

[1] Constantine Paulowitsch, Grand Duke of Russia, husband of Princess Julie.
[2] Henry LI, Prince of Reuss-Ebersdorf.

October 12th (early. Saalfeld). I drove yesterday through incessant rain, getting here at 10. Hardly had I got to sleep, when I was awakened by messages from Antoinette, containing the pleasant news that the Emperor and the Grand Duke would be arriving in Weimar at mid-day on the 14th. I am very glad to be achieving my object and to rid myself of the fear of having offended against the rules of etiquette, which to a person of my age would not be readily forgiven.

In the evening (Jena). At 11, I left Saalfeld and got here as night was falling. I drove through some very pretty country, made still more beautiful by the autumn tints. We passed through many friendly little villages. Between Kahle and Jena, the bare hilly country is less attractive, and poor burnt Jena looks very desolate.

October 14th (Weimar). I left Jena early and remembering the tragic day, which decided the fate of Germany, I was haunted on my way through the grey hills and narrow valleys by the thought of the awful scenes of carnage enacted there. Up to Weimar, the country is not pretty, — nothing but fields made famous by that fateful day of October 14. I reached Weimar at 11, which in the bright morning sun made a pleasing impression upon me. I got out at a big hotel outside the town. Everyone was on tiptoe with expectation. Soldiers were marching towards the gate at which the Emperor was due to make his entry. Officers in full dress with powder were hurrying towards the Castle, and sightseers were crowding the pavement. At 12 I paid my visit to the Duchess,[1] who received me in a most friendly and cordial manner. Her tall upright figure and her serious though not unpleasant cast of features had a certain attraction for me, being the outward sign of her temperament. The Princess[2] is not pretty, but clever. This is apparent in her decided features. On my return I found still more movement in the streets, and some of the Emperor's suite were already appearing. At ½ p.1 the ringing of the church bells announced his arrival. A detachment of French dragoons preceded the carriage and beside it rode Weimar Hussars, "Jäger," the Master of the Horse, etc. A long procession of carriages followed and the friendly sun shone on the cavalcade. Antoinette, my brother and

[1] Louise, Duchess of Saxe-Weimar, daughter of the Landgrave Louis IX of Hesse-Darmstadt.
[2] Born Princess Louise.

Leopold, who had arrived with the suite, came at once to see me.

In the evening. I end these last hours of a very fatiguing day, but though desperately tired, I am satisfied with the result of my journey. The Grand Duke only drive to the "Schloss" to take leave, and then came on to me. At first he appeared rather embarrassed, but he soon became friendly and cordial. He lunched with us and hardly had we finished with the Emperor arrived, a civil gesture which has pleased me for various reasons. His fine mild countenance has still the same expression of kindness, which is so irresistible and quite peculiar to him, but I find him aged. Seldom is a man so gifted by nature as is Alexander, certainly very few Monarchs. What a pity that these rare gifts are spoilt by a certain weakness and vanity! Constantine remained till 9 o'clock. We chatted happily together, discussing the incredible times we are living in. His judgment of the great and terrible man whom he admires, as well as of the proud frivolous people who have been so cleverly led by him, is quite correct. Constantine has knowledge of human nature. What might have been made of this young man, had he had a different upbringing, and grown up in other surroundings!

Antoinette drove off at 10 o'clock to the Ball, and I accompanied her as far as the "Schloss," which was one blaze of light. All the houses near by were brilliantly illuminated; on the same spot at the same hour, 2 years ago, houses were being burnt, and people were being slaughtered. Thus time glosses over the most awful hours and turns this sad anniversary into a gay festival, thus obliterating past miseries!

October 16th (early). At 5 o'clock yesterday, I drove to Hof for dinner, and just before that my sister-in-law[1] arrived from Ebersdorf. I found a large gathering of Princes and Gentlemen in the stately "Schloss'. It was a brilliant assembly, to which the fine rooms formed a suitable setting. Princess Stephanie of Baden with her fat, phlegmatic husband arrived shortly after me. This little French lady did not fit in very well with her surroundings, for which she was neither born nor bred, and her whole "tournure" gave evidence of it. But she is very pretty; her dark blue eyes surmounted by fine eyebrows, render her most attractive to men. Napoleon's adopted daughter might have given herself airs, and been very haughty and

[1] Louise Christine, wife of Prince Henry XLIII of Reuss Köstritz.

condescending, but here at least, she behaved in a very affable and friendly manner. Besides the Hereditary Grand Duke of Baden, the Hereditary Grand Duke of Hesse-Darmstadt was there; he was painfully "gauche" and shy, but very good-natured. The amiable Prince William of Prussia was there too, and his beaming face showed how pleased he was to be in Germany again. What must he have felt at having to spend yesterday's anniversary of the downfall of Prussia here? I also noticed the clever, pleasant Hereditary Prince of Oldenburg and the Hereditary Princes of Mecklenburg Strelitz and Homburg. The Emperor Alexander arrived a little later. It is impossible to combine kindliness with a more regal manner. No one understands better "l'apropos de la politique" and from his splendid appearance benevolence is radiated.

In the evening (Jena). After a very pleasant morning spent with my sister of Reuss Köstritz, we came on here. I shall always retain an agreeable memory of Weimar and the brilliant society I met here for the first time.

October 19th (Saalfeld). It was a difficult business, getting away to-day from Jena, as so many of the guests were leaving Weimar at the same time and they had requisitioned most of the horses in the neighbourhood. We had to wait till mid-day and even then we only secured miserable horses, who positively dragged us along at a snail's pace. A grey mist soon turned into rain and entirely obliterated the fine scenery.

October 21st (Coburg). Though in the worst weather one can imagine, Leopold and I made the journey from Saalfeld astonishingly quickly. Snow was falling in great flakes and lay thick on the trees and the ground.

November 29th. According to a letter from Szinborsky, Ernest left St. Petersburg on the 10th, expecting to arrive here in the first days of next month. I can only partially rejoice at his return, fearing that he may have left Russia without having attained his object or made any arrangements, in which case the whole journey will have been all for nothing!

December 9th (in the evening). With an aching heart I closed this day, so full of memories of my beloved one's departure from this world. I seemed to live again through every moment of that tragic day. We peacefully and reverently knelt at God's altar, taking Holy Communion in commemoration of his passing away and remembering with thankfulness all he had been to us.

December 18th. Sophie and her pretty little boy arrived safely his evening. To the pleasure of having this dear good child again with me, is added the happy expectation of also shortly seeing Julie again. I am really thankful for Antoinette that she will no longer be limited to my company. It seemed rather pitiful, that after 7 long years she should return to her old home, to find only Leopold and myself.

December 22nd. This afternoon Julie returned from her Swiss journey, looking so well and so blooming. What a joy it is to have my children returning to me one after another! After 2 lonely winters how I shall enjoy having my children around me.

December 24th. How time flies! Christmas is already here, and we shall be starting a new year in a few more days. This one with its many anxieties and joys has passed very quickly. All the children were mad with delight over their Christmas presents, but I could not help remembering former happy times, which can never return.

1809

January 1st. I am closing this first day of the new year in a somewhat depressed state of mind, having been much vexed by a letter from Ernest, who keeps putting off his return indefinitely. This is the 2nd winter I am spending in fruitless waiting and hoping against hope. I was so rejoicing at the thought of having all my children gathered around me, and owing to Ernest's absence my pleasure is much damped. I closed the old year yesterday so happily, so thankful for its calm days, and now in the very first hours of the new year, clouds again appear on the horizon.

January 16th. Victoire and her charming children arrived this evening from Schindler accompanied by Fräulein Späth and Countess Wieser.

January 17th. We spent part of the evening with Victoire, and how I enjoyed, after years, seeing my 4 daughters together, and in the same house (inhabited by Victoire) in which their happy childhood was spent. Oh! if their dear Father could only have seen this delightful gathering of children and grandchildren!

January 18th. This morning, in severe cold, Mensdorff arrived having travelled all through the wintry night, in order not to miss being with me for my birthday. I have just returned from the Casino, where Marie, her brother, Hugo and Charles performed beautiful Tableaux Vivants, forming delightful groups and then followed a very successful comedy excellently acted.

January 19th. I am full of gratitude to Providence for having bestowed so many blessings upon me and having permitted me to spend such a happy birthday, surrounded by such a big family gathering. It is the happiest birthday I have spent for years as there were no anxieties to mar anything, and I could enjoy to the full the cheerful presence of my dear grandchildren who are so full of life and fun.

January 24th. We celebrated to-day Mensdorff's birthday, by having a "déjeuner" in Ketschendorf. The centre-piece of the table was a nest of moss in which sat Hugo representing a cupid. He gave all our small gifts to his Father.

February 5th. A French officer from the General Staff, lunched to-day with us and I own that this visit filled me with forebodings. In a similar manner one of these gentlemen came down on us a few weeks before the Battle of Saalfeld, no doubt to spy out the land. To-day this man comes like a stormy petrel presaging trouble.

February 6th. It grieves me not to be able thoroughly to enjoy having Ferdinand here, but I am so oppressed by a secret dread, like the feeling that precedes a thunderstorm!
Mensdorff and Ferdinand speak with such certainty of a coming war, that I am in a perfect fever.

February 14th. It is a dreadful stormy night, one feels as if the elements were bent on destroying this world and perhaps Ernest is now on his way; this thought rather alarms me. I had been looking forward all day with such pleasure to his coming, but poor Sophie's tears this evening have quite upset me. The thought of Ferdinand and Mensdorff's imminent departure and the threat of war fill my soul with gloom.

February 15th. At 2 a.m. Ernest arrived and my ardent wish to have all my children around me is, thank God! at last fulfilled.

February 21st. The short delightful days in which all my children were gathered around me are past. How happy we were, and now I fear such a thing is not likely to happen again for many a year. I am tired out with weeping and cannot collect my thoughts. Yesterday a courier arrived calling Mensdorff away, and to-day he and Ferdinand have left to face the dangers of war!

March 5th. The French Minister in Berlin has demanded that our poor Contingent should be placed at the disposal of Marshal

Davoust. My heart aches to see these poor cheery peasant lads going, as it were, to be slaughtered! It is really dreadful that we German should be so entirely given over into the power of this uncrowned Tyrant. It will soon be seen if, in this new struggle, the deteriorated German has deserved his fate or whether some spark of their forefathers' strength and love of freedom still survives in their effeminate descendants.

March 7th. According to all the news one gets, war is inevitable. I cannot yet realise the possibility of a fresh war, and I look with horror into the terrifying future. The one thing that fills my mind is anxiety for Ferdinand and Mensdorff.

March 9th. These days are so full of nameless dread, that one's heart seems to despair of any comfort. This is my case to-day. Ernest has received orders from Paris to recall his brother from the Austrian army.

March 10th. I closed last evening with what amounted almost to deadly fear. Napoleon's order for Ferdinand's recall, and the conviction that he will not obey this order, which to him would seem dishonourable, alarms me more than ever as this might involve his being made a prisoner. I was desperate, but am no easier in my mind to-day, dwelling constantly on the worst side.

March 12th. To-day, for the last time, our officers dined with us, for to-morrow the small Contingent marches off, where to, God knows? but any way to face death. I took leave of them with an aching heart. Which of them, I wonder, will return? For any one of them to be numbered among the fallen would be very tragic.

March 13th. This morning I watched the departure of our noble little Contingent with almost as much pain as if they had been my children. The destination is quite uncertain, but they are proceeding first to Würzburg.

March 15th. The 5th Regiment of French Hussars rode through the town this morning "en parade," having previously halted on the market place. It is a fine Regiment. Later, followed the 17th Line Regiment, dead tired, with ragged shoes. They were mostly conscripts, but when absorbed into the big mass of troops will probably fight none the less well.

I am terribly perturbed and anxious at the number of French troops streaming over the borders of Austria and Bohemia. After having goaded on the lion, Austria sits back and hopes for his downfall. Oh! how worried I am about Ferdinand!

March 17th. This morning early, the 11th Regiment of the "Chasseurs-à-Cheval," one of the finest, arrived in the town. The large amounts of transport and equipment demanded and the burden of billeting and feeding these insatiable guests, means the ruin of the countries they go through. My poor country, what will become of you in this new storm! My anxiety increases daily, for I feel certain of Austria's downfall. Day and night my thoughts are with Ferdinand.

March 18th. The whole of this day has been spoilt by the expectation of Marshal Davoust's arrival, and after all, he never came. But nevertheless we received another unexpected and frightening visit. The Minister to the Rhine Confederation arrived with messages from the Emperor Napoleon to Ernest. The latter is requested to put his Contingent at the Emperor's disposal (thank God it is no longer here) and Ferdinand is to be ordered to return, which he won't and cannot do. I am afraid that somehow suspicions against Ernest have been aroused and that Bacher has been sent to have a look around. Alas! the outbreak of war is very close.

March 19th. Marshal Davoust's visit has been got over; it was a weary business trying to enliven him, for it is impossible to be more stolid and uncommunicative than was this thoroughly unpleasant man. His face betrays that he can be very harsh and brutal though not specially spiteful or intellectual. His A.D.C.s were as unamiable as the Marshal himself. This afternoon at 5, yet another Infantry Regiment passed through, and to-morrow there will be more Regiments. I cannot for a moment get rid of the idea that all these troops are moving against Austria and that Ferdinand and Mensdorff will soon be facing them.

March 20th. Troops keep coming through unceasingly. Where shall we find the means to feed these rapacious guests? This morning

Victoire accompanied her delightful children for a certain distance on their way home. I shall really miss Charles very much, for he is a dear clever boy, full of life and go. Feodore is a sweet little pickle, who already now, shows grace in every movement of her small body.

March 21st. To-day two Infantry and one Rifle Regiment marched through, 2000 men remaining in the town. Yesterday's troops behaved very badly. The huge number of relays for transport is completely ruining the poor peasants, and it presses doubly hard on them, when work in the fields has started. When I see the poor, hardly used peasant and his lean and tottering cattle I often forget my own anxieties in realising their misery. But this is only the beginning of the terrible issues which are coming upon us.

March 26th. The passage of troops still; continues; though it was supposed to end this week, we have now suddenly been over-run by the whole of St. Hilaire's Division. The burden of this constant passage of troops falls heavily upon the poor little country. The French make no difference between friend's or enemy's territory, and there are no excesses they do not permit themselves with impunity.

April 10th. This morning Victoire went away with her husband, who came on the 4th to fetch her. Poor little soul, she was loath to leave us, and her departure has grieved me doubly as she is not in good health.

April 15th. According to the newspapers, war has been declared against France, Austria having started it!

April 16th. The news that a detachment of Lancers under the command of an officer are patrolling Baireuth greatly agitates us.

April 17th. This afternoon we heard the sound of guns in the direction of Würzburg or Amberg. This is where Mensdorff is stationed. May God in His mercy protect him and grant that we may get some news of him.

April 19th. The messenger sent by Sophie to Baireuth to try to find out something about her husband, has returned without being able to fulfil his mission. It is desperate in these days of anxiety to have to continue without news. At this moment we hear that there are no French in Baireuth.

April 21st. Still no news of Mensdorff. The Austrians are said to have fallen like a whirlwind on Nürnberg and Regensburg, but this is only hearsay, and no certainty.

April 24th. A French courier has announced here to-day, that Napoleon has completely beaten the Austrians near Regensburg, Eckmühl and Straubingess. The Archduke Charles has been wounded, and his brother Ludwig and various generals are among the fallen. Dear God! I wonder where Ferdinand is now? But perhaps at this moment it is a blessing to know nothing definitely.

April 26th. With a thankful heart I retire to rest, having heard that Mensdorff is safe. I was worn out by anxiety caused by the increasingly bad news of the unlucky battle of the 21st. With anxious foreboding I broke the seal of Mensdorff's letter and was then nearly petrified by seeing the word "wounded." Thank God for having preserved his life! On the 23rd during a fierce fight between his Regiment and French "Carabiniers" he got a sword thrust in his cheek and hand, but mercifully neither wound is dangerous. I hurried to Sophie who was beyond herself with joy at the safety of her beloved husband. Now that he is removed from the danger zone, she is hurrying to Prague where he has been taken and where she will be able to nurse him. I thank God with my whole heart that Ferdinand was not in this murderous battle and that Mensdorff had a few words with him on the 23rd. I will never again, Oh God! lack faith in thy merciful protection of my fear ones or doubt its continuation.

April 27th. I heard with anxiety that guns were firing the whole of yesterday afternoon. A detachment of Saxon Hussars in charge of an officer came here to-day.

April 29th. Just as it was two years ago during those dreadful days of Prussia's downfall, news keeps coming in of one French victory after another. Of course one only hears their "bulletins," the disgustingly arrogant tone of which may well be exaggerated. Nevertheless they cannot be entirely inventions, if as they claim the

Austrians have again been defeated on the 22nd. Thank goodness Ferdinand was still all right on the 23rd, but what terrible dangers he is constantly exposed to! When I think of this, my confidence and hope are rather inclined to weaken. But God will, I am sure, forgive my looking forward with dread to the future as if it were not in His hands. A delayed letter from Mensdorff had much upset me and made me still more anxious. Her had already been wounded once before, on the 13th at Amberg, by a glancing bullet in the shoulder. Luckily it was a spent bullet and did not prevent him drawing his sword after a few days although when he was wounded the second time, the first wound was not yet healed. It is with deadly fear that I shall see this brave man return to the fighting line.

May 6th. The weather is so cold that hardly a blossom dares come out. Sophie reached her husband safely. He had seen Ferdinand on the 28th, which fact is encouraging.

May 10th. Württemberg[1] arrived quite unexpectedly this afternoon. His journey to Paris cost him a lot of money and did not help him. The foolish hope of securing Napoleon's help and obtaining reparations takes many a poor deluded German to Paris, and it generally proves to be their undoing.

May 21st. I have to-day had a long talk with Württemberg about Paris and Napoleon, and to my anxiety for Ferdinand and Mensdorff, is now added the worry that Ernest is not a "persona grata" with the mighty Ruler. Württemberg thinks that Ernest should try to win Napoleon's good graces, but goodness knows how this is to be done. Ernest will never truckle, like so many; this doubtful accomplishment is not given to everyone. In my opinion, the honest and strict carrying out of his duties is the only line of conduct an honourable man can take without disgrace. Only knaves succeed by tortuous ways, and he who cannot skate on thin ice had better keep away. If Napoleon is bent on ruining us, then nothing can save us, for there is no injustice he cannot explain away when he wishes to. If he considers that we stand in his way, he will not stir a finger for us.

[1] Alexander, Duke of Württemberg, husband of the Duchess Antoinette.

June 2nd. The Prague newspaper announces an Austrian victory, but in the midst of my joy over the news I dread Napoleon's fury, when he too experiences defeat.

June 4th. This morning Sophie returned from Prague, having travelled very quickly. She left Prague early in the morning of the 1st. Great rejoicings were going on in that town. The Austrian successes on the 21st, 22nd, and 23rd, at Aspern were very important ones. Thank God for this! Ferdinand came safely through the great dangers he was exposed to. The Austrian Infantry has one more lived up to its splendid reputation, and in spite of what the all highest may say he has received a thorough beating.

June 18th. What a happy summer this would be, were it not for this dreadful war! The thought of it spoils every enjoyment. I have now been writing this diary for 5 summers, of which not one has resembled the other. We have in fact spent quite a pleasant summer enjoying simple country diversions, Ernest at the Rosenau, Julie in her garden, Sophie and Antoinette in the town and Leopold everywhere. When Ernest is not in Coburg, I usually lunch alone at Ketschendorff, and we all meet for tea. Probably I shall have to spend next summer alone, when Antoinette will have gone again to the far north. How we shall miss her delightful company and originality. I cannot bear to think of the parting with which I am faced, and which each day is bringing nearer.

July 15th. It seems only too certain that there has been a terrible battle near the Danube. From the 3rd to the 6th firing was heard in Vienna. I fear that it is only too likely that it has proved unlucky for Austria, even discounting French lies. I feel quite at the end of my tether and, what can have happened to Ferdinand? I have no words for this anguish and can only implore God not to abandon us!

July 18th. I can hardly write, I am so upset by the news that Ferdinand has been wounded, even though, mercifully, not dangerously. God be thanked that in that desperate battle in the first days of this month, in which so many thousands lost their lives, he escaped with only a wound. On the 10th he was already in Prague.

July 19th. To-morrow Antoinette and Julie are going to Prague to visit Ferdinand and only this evening have I discovered that I might have travelled with them, if only I had made up my mind in time. How often have I, through my slowness in taking a decision, missed opportunities, which I have afterwards bitterly regretted.

July 21st. Ernest goes to-morrow to Amorbach. He is afraid of the journey to Bohemia which I so much wish to undertake, as he dreads that Napoleon with his petty dislike might put a wrong interpretation on this journey and this might prejudice Ernest's chances. Naturally that is the last thing I would wish to do, although it is very hard to have to give up my cherished desire to visit Ferdinand.

July 29th. At last I have received a letter from Ferdinand. The dear good boy managed to write to me the very day after he was wounded, but the letter has been delayed a whole fortnight on the road. On the afternoon of the 6th as his Regiment was advancing to meet the French Infantry, he was wounded in the foot, three toes being injured. What a mercy it did not hit him in the chest or head. How thankful I am to God for preserving my son, in that fearful battle.

July 30th. Sophie has received letters from Prague reporting that Ferdinand has already been out driving. His sisters arrived on the 24th, and Oh! why did I not go with him?

A rumour of peace is prevalent, and if this is confirmed that will decide my journey.

August 7th. Yesterday afternoon my daughters returned from Prague. Peace still seems very uncertain. Ferdinand is suffering a good deal from his wound, which is more serious than he gave me to understand in his letter. I have heard with horror some of the details of that terrible battle. With cool determination Ferdinand led his Regiment into the fray. Though wounded the brave boy attacked a second time, and only when his horse sank under him seriously wounded, did the pain and loss of blood overcome him. At first the surgeon dreaded that blood poisoning might supervene, the big toe being in such a bad condition, and that would have been fatal.

August 12th. Ferdinand is going to Töplitz where I shall visit him for a few days. Antoinette can only remain a few days with me, after my return, but I could not bring myself to give up my journey on that account.

August 14th (Ebersdorf). It is five years since I was last in my old home and sweet memories came to me as I drove through the well remembered countryside. Memories of my early childhood and youth. How often on just such a fine summer's evening, have I driven with my mother and sister through the Frankenwald. The long years seemed to have vanished, and I felt myself a child again, with all the joys of life in front of me. That Ebersdorf should have changed so little is a real happiness to me. It all looks just the same!

(The manuscript from this date, up to the beginning of the following year 1810, is missing.)

1 8 1 0

February 20th. At length it would seem that Napoleon's important choice has been made, and that it is to the Archduchess Marie-Louise of Austria that the hard lot has fallen. What must be the feelings of the Emperor's daughter, in mounting the throne from which Marie-Antoinette was hurled, to die under the guillotine! What a miserable though gilded future awaits the poor victim! God give her courage and wisdom, and should she have as big a heart as her ancestress Marie-Thérèse, she will find comfort in the hope of becoming the guardian angel of her native country.

February 27th. A tremendous thaw has set in, causing the roads and meadows to be inundated and unfortunately the Contingent for the Army will have to be on its way, in a very few days. These poor men have only had three months' rest since their return from imprisonment in Tyrol. It will soon be a year since they went out for the 1st time and how many have not returned!

February 28th. It has been announced in the papers that Rome has been declared a Department of France. Imperial Rome to become a Department in that Gaul which was once a Province in the far-flung Roman Empire! How low must the people have sunk, to stand such a degradation! I vain does this modern Attila aspire to make Paris the first city of the world. Fallen Rome will ever remain unique with its classic beauty crowning the seven hills, and her great dead who lie beneath her ruins will remain an inspiration for many hundred years, after Napoleon's lust to destroy all that was great and noble has been forgotten. In the same way did the Moslem destroy Greece and Byzantium in their hatred for all that was great and beautiful.

March 2nd. This morning, in terrible weather the Contingent marched off to Spain.

March 5th. I have read in the paper to-day with real sorrow, that the gallant, patriotic leader of the Tyrolese, Andreas Hofer, has been shot at Mantua. It would have been such a fine thing to have pardoned this great and simple-minded peasant! But when has our blood-stained Tyrant shown himself to be generous or kind? In years to come posterity will judge between this murderer and the lion-hearted Tyrolese.

March 16th. On Ernest's advice, Ferdinand has gone again to Vienna, to try to get some certain information as to what his future is to be. Now that the situation between Austria and France is on such an amicable footing it ought to be easy for Ferdinand to obtain permission from the Emperor Napoleon to continue serving in the Army. But that the German Princes, once so free, should have themselves forged the chains which bind them to the arbitrary will of this foreign Despot and necessitates their asking favours from him, in a humiliation to which I can never accustom myself!

March 18th. I am quite cheered up to-day by a piece of news which renders Ferdinand and Mensdorff very happy. They have both received the Cross of the Thérèsian order. This order is the pride of every Austrian combatant, as it can only be given for great personal valour and in no wise depends on any favouritism from the Monarch, but entirely on the recommendation of men who have fought and suffered together.

March 31st. Ferdinand has been in Prague for 3 months, and we have been waiting for him in vain. Since the 9th, when he went to Vienna, we have not had a word from him!

April 5th. To-morrow I am going to Gera, and I hope to goodness I shall find Ferdinand here, on my return, for my patience is getting exhausted.

April 13th. I was somewhat surprised to find on getting up, that the whole countryside was covered with snow, as in winter. At half-past six I drove out of Saalfeld and passing through the forest it was still so cold that the windows of my carriage were frozen over. The road was good so that I got here this evening at half-past six, and was delighted to find Ferdinand, who is very nearly quite recovered and looks flourishing and cheerful.

May 25th. I am about to gratify a long-cherished wish of visiting Switzerland, but as usual on starting a journey, my pleasure is somewhat marred by a feeling of apprehension. Ferdinand and Leopold are accompanying me.

July 14th (Coburg). At midnight I got back here. It was a mistake in this heat to try to cover such a long distance in one day. It was a lovely evening when we passed through Bamberg, where the town was very animated, and the moonlit night as bright as day, showed us the pleasant countryside. The smell of hay still lingered in the meadows.

Everyone is already at the Rosenau, but Sophie, her husband and children came here at once. Hugo has grown astonishingly, and a little black eyed Alphonse looks as fresh as a rosebud.

July 21st. I am feeling very sad at the thought that in another two days, Ferdinand will be leaving for the depths of Hungary. In a few months Leopold will also be leaving us, to find in the far north the fulfilment of his hopes and wishes.

July 25th. I read to-day in the paper of the death of the good and amiable Queen of Prussia.[1] I did not know that she had been dangerously ill. She was too good for this world and one of the best queens imaginable. This most attractive person, with her beautiful expressive eyes, won all hearts. How I pity the poor unhappy King for having lost such a wife!

August 24th. Hugo is four to-day, God bless the dear good little boy, who is such a charming child, so clever and lovable. May the Almighty lead him safely through the perils of life and keep his heart gentle and pure.

September 26th. Mensdorff has become Colonel of the Lancer Regiment "Archduke Charles," and poor Sophie's pleasure at her

[1] Louise, b. 1776, wife of King Frederick William III. Their nine children included Kings Frederick William IV and William I, the latter becoming German Emperor in 1871.

husband's honourable preferment is quite spoilt by the thought of the impending separation.

October 3rd. Mensdorff left this morning to join his Regiment in Moravia. May God's blessing go with him!

October 6th. There is nothing more fatiguing than a state visit. It entails such a lot of rushing about, idle talk, dressing up, and what not! One day like that seems like ten others. The whole Court of Hildburghausen, with the Crown Prince's bride,[1] passed through here to-day on their way to Munich, and dined with us. The future Crown Princess of Bavaria is charming, so graceful and pretty; her whole personality radiating benevolence and kindness.

October 11th. In a couple of days, Sophie with Hugo will be leaving for Amorbach and Leopold for Paris. Parting with the latter, for this journey, which will be followed by a much longer one, causes me much pain. I find it difficult to conceal my depression.

October 13th. Sophie and Leopold left very early this morning, on a beautiful autumn day.

November 3rd. What a fright I got this morning on opening and reading a letter from Ferdinand, written in a very shaky hand and telling me of his having again fallen a victim to that horrid Hungarian fever, which so nearly cost him his life, last time.

November 7th. To-day Ernest had a letter from Ferdinand, which has quite set my mind at rest. He must be nearly recovered if he could write such a long letter, and I am so thankful.

November 8th. Both in the political and physical world, these are very dark, drab days. The dreary, foggy ones of late autumn already tend to make one depressed, to which is now added the feeling of sorrow for so many unfortunate people so hardly hit by Napoleon's tyrannical decree as to the Colonial produce. With an iron hand

[1] Thérèse, Princess of Saxe-Hildburghausen.

thousands of poor defenceless people are being ruined and my heart aches for them. The Despot might choose to forbid people like us having coffee and any other Indian luxuries, but to the masses this arbitrary order that has gone forth, deprives them of their means of subsistence. What compensation is there for the poor cotton spinners, who have now lost their employment and must starve?

November 11th. Leopold has written such a gloomy letter from Paris, hinting that there was fresh trouble brewing, that my anxiety and alarm are increasing from day to day. What measures may this human tormentor be again devising! When will the thundercloud which is gathering burst upon us? Lucky are those who can flee for safety to free, happy Albion!

November 21st. Quite unexpectedly Ernest returned to-day from Paris and this sudden arrival filled me with alarm and forebodings, which proved to be only too justified. Leopold must quit the Russian Army. To this I could reconcile myself, for I am convinced that no good will come to us from the North. But he will now probably have to enter the French service! I had not prepared myself for this contingency. Of all dreadful possibilities, this has always been my greatest dread, and now I fear the dread is likely to be fulfilled. Oh God! to what dangers of every possible kind, will his youth not be exposed! Napoleon has said: "Si le Prince Léopold va en Russie, je chasserai le Duc." What, however, is this inhuman injustice to him, when he has determined on our destruction? There is no doubt that he is very ill disposed towards us.

November 26th. Mensdorff came this evening, but for the first time his arrival has not given me the usual pleasure. The dreadful decree that obliges every French subject to leave the Austrian Army and return to Napoleon's iron rule, affects also Mensdorff, and he has come to discuss matters with his wife.

December 4th. To-morrow Leopold is starting for Dresden and Berlin, and soon after his return here, he will; have to go again to Paris. I envisage this journey and his whole future with a nameless dread. God grant that I may be worrying myself unnecessarily.

December 12th. Mensdorff leaves us again to-morrow to meet his uncertain future.

December 26th. Leopold has returned this evening. He has succeeded in obtaining the St. John's cross (Johanniter-Kreuz). This venerable order of Knighthood, whose foundation dates from the time of the Crusades, is now also to cease. The big revenues amassed by the Order are to be surrendered to the Crown, which owing to Napoleon's spoliation is badly in need of funds. Thus disappears from the earth, everything that is ancient and revered.

The spirit of Chivalry no longer fits in with our present egotistical times, when success is all that is cared for and seems to flourish.

December 31st. It is with a peculiar satisfaction that I am spending these last hours of the departing year alone. With deep gratitude to God for all His goodness to me, I bear in mind how He preserved my children in their hours of great danger. I shall always look back with pleasure and satisfaction to the pleasant summer I spent and the delightful trip to Switzerland. Alas! that with the fine months of the year all my peace of mind should have vanished! Added to my anxiety regarding Leopold's future, is the regret that Ferdinand is obliged to leave his Regiment.

At the age of twenty-five he is now deprived of any occupation, or prospects of an interesting career.

Augusta, Duchess of Saxe-Coburg-Saalfeld

Francis, Duke of Saxe-Coburg-Saalfeld

Ernest, Duke of Saxe-Coburg Gotha

Francis, Prince of Saxe-Coburg-Saalfeld

1 8 1 1

January 7th. Leopold leaves to-night. I cannot express my feelings; it is as if all hope were gone! Napoleon's pronouncement has ruined all the poor boy's prospects. His dearest hopes and plans have always been centred in Russia and now they have vanished like a morning mist.

January 18th. I have had a great joy, Ferdinand came this morning, as usual without warning. He is looking very well.

February 8th. Ferdinand has sent in his papers and leaves with a heavy heart the regiment in which he had known so much happiness, and in which he was so popular and so much respected. I suffer with and for him, my only comfort being that owing to his late illness and wounds, he now needs a rest. He has carried away with him many expressions of regret from officers and men which he values very much. But I pity Leopold even more, whose hopes and ambitions are nipped in the bud. Ferdinand can at least comfort himself with the thought that he had gained distinction in the war, and whatever his future career may be, he will always have the battles of Aspern and Wagram to his credit. Poor Leopold, on the other hand, has had no chance of distinguishing himself, and his wings are for ever clipped.

March 23rd. Leopold arrived unexpectedly today, still as free as when he left. For this I am deeply thankful and it has taken a load off my mind.

March 24th. It is much the same with joy and bad luck; they rarely come singly. Mensdorff has now also arrived. It does me good to see the brothers reunited. Seldom were brothers greater friends, and in such complete agreement. This harmony is the joy of my life.

April 10th. Ferdinand has to-day received his papers signed by the General and with it the promise that should he at any time in the future wish, and be permitted, to rejoin, he could be reinstated! I wonder if this will ever happen.

May 16th. My sons have gone to Dresden and Sophie and her husband to Moravia, leaving their sweet little boy behind, as my only companion.

June 11th. My peaceful enjoyment of the glorious spring weather has been interrupted by a letter from Sophie. Mensdorff is to continue to serve, and all my beautiful plans to have Sophie and her children with me have been dashed to the ground. The Emperor Francis, when Mensdorff paid him his farewell visit, told him he need not resign and that all was arranged! Though Napoleon would not alter his ruling regarding every French subject, he was willing at the Emperor Francis's request, to make an exception for Mensdorff. He, of course, as anyone else would have done in a similar position, agreed to remain.

July 5th. The fragments of our poor little Contingent have returned from Spain – 18 men out of 250! Most of the losses were not due to actual fighting, but chiefly to diseases, scarcity, and neglect, added to the hardships caused by the Spanish climate; and now the poor weary men have found their last resting place in foreign soil. Half the town turned out to meet the survivors.

July 19th (Lobenstein). I came here to-day in the most unbearable heat. Twenty years have gone by since I was last in this house which in my childhood and youth I often visited. It is now a most friendly and pleasant house, presided over by a very amiable young woman, Franziska, Pss. Reuss-Lobenstein.[1] She has brought life and grace into what was formerly rather a dreary house, only inhabited by men.

July 29th (Töplitz). I have been resting after yesterday's journey here, from Eger, and I have not paid any visits. In the afternoon I went into the Gardens, which were teaming with people, but I did

[1] Franziska, Pss. Reuss-Lobenstein, daughter of Prince Henry XLII of Reuss Köstritz.

not see one known face. The first days in a watering place, when one knows no one and no one interests one, are always rather trying and almost make one wish to leave again at once.

July 30th. I had intended calling on Princess Solms[1] to-day but she came to see me this morning with her brother the Hereditary Grand Duke of Mecklenburg Strelitz. She talked incessantly and tearfully about the death of the beloved and unforgettable Queen Louise.

August 24th. How quickly the time passes by. This is already the last day of my stay here. The four weeks have gone like a dream and I have really spent them very pleasantly. I have been favoured with lovely weather, and have made many agreeable acquaintances, whose society I have enjoyed, and I have not had one moment's boredom. Surely at my age one cannot expect more from a watering place. I like the country round here very much, and this afternoon after endless farewell visits, I went up to my favourite hill, from which there is such a beautiful view.

August 30th (Coburg). In the same lovely weather, I got back here this evening. The gentlemen of the party returned from Pyrmont on the 20th. It suited Ernest but Ferdinand looks far from well. My sister-in-law Caroline[2] arrived yesterday from Gandersheim and it has given me much pleasure to see her again. The times have dealt hardly and devastatingly with her simple life, and the institution to which she belonged has been closed down after 1000 years!

September 20th. At last I have paid my visit to Seidenstadt, which is always a long business. I was glad to find the Hereditary Grand Duchess of Mecklenburg Strelitz still there, whose friendship I value so much.

October 17th. This has been a long day and I shall not quickly forget how intensely boring it was. Ernest had begged us to come to Rodach,

[1] Frederica, wife of Prince Frederick William of Solms Brannfels, daughter of the reigning Duke Charles of Mecklenburg Strelitz and widow of Prince Ludwig of Prussia. He married in 1816 Ernest Augustus, Duke of Cumberland.
[2] Caroline Ulrika Amalia, Princess of Saxe-Coburg-Saalfeld.

where members of the Hildburghausen family were expected. The morning was fine and we got there by 12 o'clock – rather too early.

All the gentlemen were out shooting with their host[1] and at half-past two the Duchess, Princess Louise,[2] and Princess George[3] arrived, accompanied by two ladies in waiting. Up to then the time had passed fairly bearably, but with the advent of these ladies, it became a hard job to entertain the company for three hours! One would need to be French to be able to carry on indefinitely a conversation all about nothing; we found it almost beyond our powers.

October 27th. I lunched to-day with Caroline at Ketschendorf. As we were sitting near the window watching a curtain of rain which hid the landscape, a carriage drawn by post horses came down the road, followed by another – it was Julie, whom we had not expected so soon. I was overjoyed at seeing her again after the lapse of a year and a half.

November 2nd. This has been a long day. There was a big "déjeuner dinatoire," in celebration of Julie's arrival, and in the evening, there was a concert. I have grown old without being able to understand why every happy event should be celebrated by some tedious entertainment.

November 30th. In spite of fog and rain Ernest went out shooting, returning as usual dead tired with his sporting friends. The damp weather and rough going always alarm me for Ferdinand's sake. After every shoot his wounded foot becomes very painful and yet he insists on accompanying the others. Oh! these men who will never deny themselves anything that amuses them!

December 31st. Already another year gone by, and astonishingly rapidly. It has not been marked by any special incidents, but I can thank God for many untroubled, tranquil days, and many untold mercies. With confidence in His protection, I shall go forward to meet the new year. Whether it will be a stormy or peaceful one, likes in Thy hands, oh God! I do not want to know anything beforehand and await the future calmly.

[1] Frederick, Duke of Saxe-Hildburghausen.

[2] Louise, Princess of Saxe-Hildburghausen.

[3] Probably the widowed Princess George of Hesse-Darmstadt, b. Countess of Leiningen-Heidesheim.

1 8 1 2

January 18th. I have spent such a happy birthday! Ernest made a real festival of it. We lunched with Julie, and drove out to the Rosenau in the afternoon in sledges, remaining for dinner. It was a stormy evening and on our return drive the torches would not burn. We took tea in Ernest's room before the Rout, and then went to the "Riesentsaal" which was in darkness and where I was asked to sit down. Suddenly a Band struck up a march, and a procession of little people headed by eight small torch bearers entered the Hall. It was quite a fairy scene. All were dressed in old-fashioned costumes, and none was over ten years old. The torch bearers, in black and red, were followed by a herald, who in a charming "couplet" asked permission for the little procession to bring its gifts. Then appeared the King and Queen in old French costumes, the pages bearing their train and purple mantle being hardly three years old. They really looked too sweet for words. Lastly came the Knights and Ladies, with their retinue and minstrels etc. More torch bearers closed the procession, in which more than thirty children took part, all unusually pretty and well got up. They went through the Hall and rooms three times and finally disbanded amidst shouts of glee.

February 20th. Our little company of soldiers paraded here for the last time before setting off to-morrow. As usual the poor things have come in for a thaw. Goodness knows to what misery and horrors they may not be exposed, in this northern war!

March 6th. We shall not be the only ones to be affected by these movements of troops and we are now expecting the Württemberg contingent, who are to await orders here.

March 14th. I have written to-day to Antoinette, hélas! Perhaps for the last time, for some while, and this makes me very sad. I wonder if letters can still get through? I have already for some time not ventured to send letters by Riga, and how long will it be possible via Austria?

The peoples of all nations are moving northwards like a devastating stream, and one feels as one would before the eruption of a volcano. This is already the fourth war in seven years, of which we have seen the outbreak in Germany.

March 29th (Easter Sunday). It is blowing and raining mercilessly – such a pity on this day, when we commemorate the resurrection of Our Lord, we would wish to see the bright sun shining on the graves of those who will also arise one day! I have always thought it a very touching custom in the Greek Church, for those who have lost their dear ones to watch the first rays of the sun over their graves on the first Easter morning after their death. How it must make them realise the evanescence of all earthly troubles!

May 20th. M . . ., coming from Kulmbach, told us that she had seen Napoleon arrive at Baireuth. The town was illuminated, etc. I am disgusted at the way in which he is always and everywhere received, and the marks of honour shown to him. If only the Germans would bear their subjugation with dignity instead of positively grovelling to the Despot, who will only further enslave them!

May 22nd. My sons are in Dresden, since the 15th, and many Sovereigns are assembled there.

June 8th. The travellers have returned to-day from Dresden. Ferdinand cannot get over the impression Napoleon's arrival made on him. He came like the Prince of Darkness on a stormy night, when the torches would hardly burn. Flashes of lightning lit the sky, and peals of thunder mixed with the half-hearted cheers of the populace, and the ghostly ringing of bells. It was an intensely interesting journey at a very critical time, and not the least interesting point was the contrast between the two Emperors. The very human Emperor Franz with his friendly courteous bearing, and Napoleon decidedly curt and rude, though possibly not intentionally, but over-elated by his extraordinary luck and cleverness. He was only affable to his Father-in-law and the King of Prussia of whom he makes use. The adulation and sickening flattery with which he is everywhere received, further increases the contemptuous, harsh attitude peculiar to him. Napoleon was not unfriendly to Ernest and the Austrian Emperor most affable. Ferdinand, of whom he spoke with high appreciation, was by his orders attached to him at F.

August 28th. With sadness I am thinking that to-day is Antoinette's birthday. I wonder where she will be spending it? And in what anxiety and trepidation? These thoughts upset me very much. But she is in Thy hands, oh Heavenly Father, and under Thy care! Hear my prayer for her, on this her birthday! Hélas! I cannot even write my good wishes to her, all communication with Russia being interrupted.

October 3rd. The French are in Moscow! That too, oh God! Now that country has also been delivered into the Destroyer's hands. Napoleon's flag will be flying from the ancient Kremlin! Thy ways are wonderful, but only what Thou willest comes to pass, and in these terrible days, that thought is my only comfort. In due time Thou wilt destroy them and scourge them with the rod of Thy anger. I will put my faith and hope in thee.

October 13th. Thank God! I have at last received a letter from Antoinette, which came through Sweden to Carlsruhe. It made my heart beat to see her handwriting again. She and her children were still well on the 12th of September, and judging from her discreetly worded letter, she was not at the moment in any alarm. May God continue to protect her!

October 22nd. This morning Mensdorff arrived to the great joy of his wife and sons. Thank God he is now removed from the dangers of the war, and can supervise the education of his charming boys. The glory of the service to which he was so devoted has now departed. The brave Austrian warriors no longer fight for their Fatherland; as French auxiliary troops they have to help with the subjection of a fine people. Under these circumstances and with his strong feelings and convictions, he found it impossible to continue serving.

November 19th. Napoleon is leaving Moscow! The "communiqués" resound with praise for his cleverness and moderation and say that it is out of love for his soldiers that he is returning to a milder climate. With what baffled rage must the would-be world conqueror have been obliged to leave Moscow which Rostopschin had delivered to the flames. Even Napoleon must now realise that he is surely a human being, capable like other mortals of error and false judgment. Even to him the Lord of Hosts will say: "Thus far, and no further!" One cannot foresee what the results of this war will be.

December 21st. The Emperor Napoleon has fled like a ghost through Germany on his way to Paris. It is a similar flight to that from Spain and the earlier flight from Egypt; he does this in order not to compromise the belief in his invincibility and to enable him to say of his Generals; "Voyez, comme ces gens se laissent battre, quand je n'y suis pas!" Or is he trying to escape from the inclemency and the hardships of a Russian winter? About this the Paris newspapers will undoubtedly feed us with inaccuracies, but it will be hard to convince us that this campaign has been so lucky and so crowned with laurels as the former ones. It would be a very salutary lesson for him, to realise that he is neither infallible nor invincible, if it did not entail the misery and death of hundreds of thousands.

December 23rd. It is now quite clear why Napoleon returned in such a hurry to Paris. His invincible army is not only beaten but annihilated, owing to the cold and lack of every kind of supplies. Never, except in Egypt, were the victorious legions in such a deplorable condition, and he hurries to Paris, abandoning his broken and luckless army, in order to take measures to avert possible further dangers, that may threaten his crown. Assuredly Nemesis will sooner or later overtake the culprit, though he may never be aware that fate is punishing him for the unhappiness brought not only to a few men but to whole nations, by sacrificing thousands to the prosecution of his unrighteous wars.

December 28th. From all sides comes news of the beaten and scattered French Armies and there are fearful stories of their sufferings and losses, due to the severities of the Russian winter and the completer breakdown of supplies. In ordinary times of peace, one is painfully affected by the death of even one person, but it is impossible even to grasp the magnitude of this holocaust of thousands who have fallen on the field of honour, amidst untold sufferings.

1813

January 2nd. May God's richest blessing rest on Ernest this day, and for the remainder of his life! May he be as happy as he deserves and Thou oh Heavenly Father! watch over him during this year, which is such an important one for him and protect him from the storms which must inevitably beset us. Give him wisdom and luck in his undertakings. We lunched with Julie, whose big room had been darkened and was decorated with little orange trees and flowers and lit up with lanterns. This had a charming effect. We had luncheon with Uncle; the Princes of Hildburghausen also came, returning afterwards to their own home. In the evening there were Tableaux Vivants which were most successful. All were done from English prints of Shakespeare's "Romeo and Juliet."

January 3rd. News has come of our poor Contingent, which has again been almost annihilated in the North, just as it was, two years ago, in Spain. Soon all Germany's youth will be lying under the sod, not having fallen in the service of their country but having been sacrificed to the insatiable love of conquest of the Usurper.

January 5th. Ernest has decided to go to Berlin in order to discover what he can about the important things that are happening, for no accurate information penetrates as far as here.

January 6th. Early this morning Ernest, Ferdinand and Hardenbrock left for Berlin, Leopold and Mensdorff accompanying them as far as Saalfeld.

January 18th. My brother and my sister-in-law arrived this evening, both looking well. This nice visit comes as a delightful birthday gift.

January 19th. I spent this day very cheerfully and happily. Ernest and Ferdinand have not yet returned. Last year Sophie was missing on my birthday, and the year before, Julie. I wonder when I shall next have all my children together. I am delighted to have my brother and sister-in-law for to-day. I suppose it is rather childish to make such a fuss about my birthday, but I always celebrate it with very mixed feelings. So many of my fear ones have gone who used to make it such a joyous day. We lunched with Julie, and in the evening we saw again two of the Tableaux, followed by a little French play, which surprised and amused me very much. The performers were Leopold and Mensdorff, who were acting for the first time and were doing it very well.

January 26th. Ernest and Ferdinand came back yesterday in good time, having made the journey from Berlin astonishingly quickly. In spite of the cold, they travelled day and night. The political situation in the north is, it seems, not quite settled. Russia is sparing Austria as much as possible, but these belated concessions are due to fear, false policy and crooked ways, as well as to the wish to paralyse the German Princes. The sly tyrant judges the moment opportune for talking revenge and drawing the fetters still closer. Never has his army been so thoroughly beaten as at this moment, and what he blazed out with such bombast in the Austrian war: "L'Armée d'Autriche a cessé d'éxister," has in an extraordinarily short time proved word for word true of his own army! How can his conscience be quite in abeyance, with so many thousands of lives sacrificed to his insane ambition? What would I not give to red his inner thoughts. If he will ever awake from his mad dream of power, God only knows, Who has permitted him to become the scourge of the nations of the earth.

January 27th. My brother left this morning. In the evening two Württemberg Officer came to tea. Both were in that fearful unbelievable retreat from Moscow, which was more like a flight. They had witnessed war with all its most ghastly destruction of human life, all, only to gratify the ambition of one man. The details are simply revolting, and I cannot bring myself to put them down. The picture of these poor helpless victims never leaves me, night or day.

February 2nd. The French are again crowing and bragging, making assurances with the greatest effrontery that they had beaten the Russians and had only retreated on account of the climatic conditions. All these boastings are no doubt intended to throw dust in the eyes of the French as to their huge losses. And this they will probably be successful in doing, but one cannot help being irritated when one reds about it. The Russians are delaying and haggling. If they left the winter go by, that restless active brain will, whilst his enemy is deliberating, seek to create a new army. Napoleon's genius will bring about fresh successes and Germany will be likely to become once more the theatre of war. What will then be the fate of our poor Country?

February 8th. There are days in our lives when one's poor tormented heart feels as if it must break. If I could complain of what is upsetting me, I should feel better, but no one must know, or have the slightest suspicion of Leopold's plans. He want to go to Munich and Vienna and from there to risk taking a very decided step. I have, as it were, been awakened out of sleep by a thunder-clap, so alarmed have I been at his plan. It is one of those matters in which there is a great deal to be said for and against. I can only see the dangers to which he is going to expose himself and I feel like shedding tears unceasingly. Another week, and he will exchange his freedom and his peaceful existence for an insecure, unknown fate. With a nameless dread I am awaiting the moment of parting. I shall miss my dear son, at every turn. Oh God! I pray for courage, faith, and hope, which on former anxious occasions Thou hast in Thy mercy granted!

February 15th. In order to celebrate her brother's impending departure, Julie gave a big tea party, and to-morrow we anticipate a visit from the Hildburghausen family which I am sure incommodes the Duchess as much as it does us. There is no more foolish form of civility than a ceremonial visit, which worries both parties and entails waste of time and money. Why people should impose this strain, on themselves, when it only leads to boredom, I cannot think.

February 16th. The Duchess[1] and Princess Louise, with their suite arrived at six in terrible weather and we had to spend the livelong

---

[1] Duchess of Hildburghausen.

evening together, trying to find subjects of conversation, which often failed us. Julie joined us at tea, after which there was a concert, followed by a supper. Now that this is all over, I cannot help deploring that the visit should have been broken in on our last quiet days before Leopold's departure.

February 19th. The Duchess left yesterday after luncheon and it was ages before they were ready to start. I really could hardly bear it, I had such a headache. The Duchess, as usual, was very kind and "polie," but although I try, I cannot find much pleasure in her society.

February 21st. I ought not to have gone to the concert, for music affects me painfully, when I am already depressed, and I could with difficulty restrain my tears. Only a few more days left before Leopold's departure, and in these last hours, the dear good fellow is only thinking of me and my affairs, trying to leave everything in order. May God bless him for it and protect him on his important errand, which is to decide the whole course of his life. There is a certain worried look in his dear face, he tries to conceal that he is leaving with a heavy heart, but I can see it – nothing escapes a mother's eye!

February 22nd. It was a beautiful day to-day and as warm as Spring. We lunched again for the first time since last Autumn at Ketschendorf, and afterwards went on foot into the town. Leopold was lunching with us for the last time, and God knows for how long. This thought saddened me very much. Early this morning there was a rumour that the Russians had got beyond Berlin and had dispersed the French army; the Prussian youth is mobilising with noble patriotism and it is to be hoped that the whole of Germany will follow their example and shake off the fetters which bind the Fatherland.

February 24th. Leopold leaves to-morrow and Ferdinand will accompany him as far as Vienna. May God's blessing go with them.

March 18th. It is a long time since I have made any entries into my Diary and even now I can hardly manage to write, I have such pain in my eyes! It is already a fortnight since my sons left. Time flies in our sad hours, as well as in our happy ones. Physical pain prevented me during the first week after the parting with my sons from giving myself over entirely to my sorrow. Never in my life have I had such unbearable pain in my head.

March 25th. In the letter I got from Leopold to-day, he tells me that he is going to the Russian Army. I felt all along that this would happen, but the certainty has hit me like a blow. The great step has now been taken which will decide his future, and he has thought it well out. May it prove to be for his happiness and may God protect and bless this dearly beloved boy.

March 27th. The Russians have penetrated at certain points as far as the Elbe, and are since the 22nd in Dresden. Ney is in Würzburg. I have again the same oppressive feeling of dread as in the year 1806, when the French hordes first overran northern Germany. With what fury will not the humiliated proud French revenge themselves on us and extinguish our dawning hopes. Never has our position been a more dangerous one than at the moment, but constant anxiety has deadened all feeling and it is with cold resignation that one awaits the worst.

March 30th. To-day was a beautiful spring day, with a shimmering blue haze shrouding the distance. These first warm days are so enheartening, but they make one very tired.

The Russians are in Leipzig, and Poles coming from various parts should be passing through here on their way to Würzburg. It is to be hoped that they will lose no time. About 700 men arrived this morning in Saalfeld, and it is said were followed by Russians. I am terribly alarmed lest there may be clashes, should they overtake them here.

How strangely things have turned out since the beginning of this year, of which we have only got through a quarter. The Russians have already reached the centre of Germany, they come as liberators to free us from the French yoke. Perhaps it is God's will, that these chains which press so hardly on us should at last be removed. But I dare not yet believe that this may happen. Oh God! Thou wilt decide as is best for us.

March 31st. This afternoon there came an A.D.C. from Maréchal Ney, wishing to speak with Ernest. The advent of this stormy petrel reminded me painfully of the autumn of 1806 when constantly such gentlemen were descending upon us, with some ulterior motive. This A.D.C. brought the Maréchal's compliments, and expressed the wish to purchase horse. He made many enquiries and told us probably many lies, such as that the Prince de la Moscova had proceeded against the Russians with 80,000 men and the Emperor with 100,000. It is very wrong at once to give way to despair, but the past has left such terrible memories, that everything that reminds one of those days makes one feel hopeless.

April 3rd. There are rumours of the sounds of firing having been heard. I close each evening with fears for what the next day may bring, particularly as Maréchal Ney's Corps d'Armée will be marching through here. But what terrifies me more than anything is St. Aignan announcing loudly that Ernest has anti-French tendencies. Is it possible that he can know where Leopold has gone to? Oh God! preserve us in this oppressive situation!

April 5th. Yesterday Cossacks and a Prussian Hussars entered Saalfeld in order to take over a French Commando there. Always in this miserable war which has been so destructive to Germany's fate, the Prussian Hussars have been the first soldiers to get there. May their appearance at this moment be a signal for the freeing of Germany from her bonds. I both rejoice at, and dread their appearing here, especially as the people are rather indiscreet in their perhaps too hopeful outlook, for which it is yet too early days.

April 8th. On a beautiful day we have been lunching with Julie at the Rosenau and we spent and enjoyed a long while out of doors, in the delicious spring sun. At this moment I receive a few lines from Leopold, who, thank God! reached his destination safely.

April 10th. It has been a regular May day and I spent the whole afternoon with Caroline at Ketschendorf, walking home across the meadows. The calm evening gave me a certain feeling of melancholy. Whilst we are enjoying this lovely spring, great armies are setting forth to fight one another. Any calamity is possible and soon death and destruction may come to us! 10,000 men are coming into the town to-morrow. The Russians are stationed on the other side of the forest, and I await with terror bloody encounters. I cannot express my feelings but I live in a constant state of passive alarm. I cannot fix my thoughts on anything pleasant, because the future seems so dark and dreary, and everything is wrapped in uncertainty. Only one thing is certain and makes my hair stand on end, and that is that we shall have to bear the burden of the billeting arrangements. General Marchand's Headquarters are here and with "la mort dans l'âme" we shall have to see and entertain these people, trying to hide our feelings. It will be no light task!

April 12th. I went rather early to Ketschendorf where we lunched. General Marchand, an elderly man, came riding by; his horses and transport did not look as if he had enriched himself much by pilfering. Later, followed a Regiment of Prince Primas also without guns. They had a good appearance.

April 20th. To-morrow Bertrand's Division is expected here, which is composed of French and Italians. I rather dread its arrival. The General was an A.D.C. of the Emperor's; this fact promises vexations of all kinds. The calm of to-day — after the departure of our recent guests — has been most acceptable and I went for a walk in the afternoon, in order to enjoy my freedom.

April 21st. Thank God! that this uneasy restless day has come to an end! Everything is quiet now, only the challenging sentries the watch-fires of the pickets are left to remind us of the dreadful invasion. Already last night, to the alarm of the inhabitants, who had not expected them so soon, 2,000 men turned up. This morning, I drove with Sophie to Ketschendorf, and troops were marching by uninterruptedly. First came two Regiments of Infantry, of which one was Italian, and then an Italian Cavalry Regiment. At 12 we drove home, and saw drawn up on the road the last arrivals of Artillery and Italian "Chasseurs." The cavalry men were lying down near their tired, scraggy horses, making a picture which could well have illustrated some tale of robber bands. They and their poor animals lay quite exhausted. Till 2 o'clock the roll of the drums of the regiments marching through, sounded ceaselessly. Since 1806, the town has not had to bear such a crushing amount of billeting, the number of troops for whom quarters had to be found being up to the last moment uncertain. This resulted in many having to make their own dispositions outside the town. All this made for disorder, and rendered everything doubly difficult. Huge requisitions have already been made, which baffle all description. The "Commissaires" will no doubt quarrel among themselves, but it is the wretched population that will suffer. I am so upset and annoyed at being so powerless to help the poor people, in their misery at having to be deprived of all they themselves need. If the troops were to stay much longer, the poorer classes would starve!

April 24th. This has been a quiet day, salutary to one's nerves. This morning the Italians marched away, after having during the night brought in a number of cattle and sheep, which they had pilfered. The lack of discipline amongst the Italians is such, that no General can keep them in bounds. The "Commissaires" are just as furious about it as we are, for soon the Army will be in absolute want, owing to their wild disorder and waste. What a dreadful prospect for us, who have still to expect 25,000 men.

April 28th. To-day highly-placed Generals again lunched with us and during the whole day troops have been uninterruptedly coming and going.

April 30th. It rained during the whole of the night, and is still doing so. In this weather a French and an Italian Regiment were camped in the meadows outside the town, there not being a hole there to accommodate them. Never has the tyrant been followed on his terrible way by more execration than now. He has rushed ahead of his troops, with reckless haste, making no provision for their needs, the result being that they are swarming over Germany like a plague of locusts and devastating everything that comes in their way. The worst of all being, that they take from the farmers and peasants the teams of oxen so indispensable to them for their work on the land.

May 4th. A French courier has come through, with the news of a battle having been won, causing the loss of 40,000 Russians and Prussians. This is probably not exact, nevertheless the bare thought of our losing a battle has greatly upset me. What a beginning! Oh Father in Heaven! hast Thou quite forsaken us, and must we give up all hope of being saved! When I look out of my window, into the lovely warm May night full of delicious spring scents, I am overwhelmed with sorrow. Nature is so beautiful and festive at this season, that it seems incredible that men should be killing one another, and that hunger and the horrors of war should be rampant in our poor land of Saxony.

May 7th. We still have only incomplete accounts of the disastrous battle of Lutzen on the 2nd. There where once Gustavus Adolphus fell, many another brave warrior has gone to his account. One does not yet know exactly what happened, but it is obvious that we must again have been overwhelmed by superior numbers. The news of the great losses, and the devastation of the countryside, weighs heavily upon one's heart. The uncertainty as to whether Leopold was there or not, does not leave me a moment's peace.

May 11th (Ketschendorf). I have been beguiled by the glorious weather into coming to stay in this dear little house, but not with the same pleasure as last year, when I was here with Leopold. I still have no definite news about him. I only know that nothing had happened to him in those first dreadful days of this month. Thank God for this! But what may not have happened to him afterwards? There are rumours of a second battle on the 6th.

May 21st. Surely it will soon have rained sufficiently, though it has been a great boon after the long drought. The trees have never had finer foliage. We must thank God for the prospect of a fine harvest, which is now so important. The French, as usual, are destroying everything they cannot eat, and Napoleon cannot or will not stop this state of things, which will undoubtedly some day recoil on his own armies. A French "Commissaire" was heard to say here: "l'indiscipline de nos troupes fera notre perte." It is so long since I had any news of Leopold, and this worries me unspeakably. I cannot understand why he has not been able to write through Bohemia. I get into a dreadful state, when I think of all the awful possibilities that may occur, and I have not a moment's peace.

May 25th. On the 19th, 20th and 21st there was a dreadful battle near Bautzen which again turned out badly for the Allies. A Württemberg Courier, who came through last night, brought the news, and ever since, I have been living in the greatest state of alarm about Leopold. I really can hardly bear this uncertainty.

May 29th. Julie lunched with us at the Rosenau and we took tea in the charming little "Wasserhäuchen" at Deslau. The weather was glorious, and the country quite lovely, but one was not in a frame of mind to be able to enjoy it. What with Ferdinand and Mensdorff discussing their plans and their future journey as well as my anxiety concerning Leopold, I cannot keep my mind at rest. God knows how our troubles will end, especially now, when Napoleon has every right to resent lour attitude. With so many other worries, I have not hitherto concentrated on this aspect of the question, but it is obviously a very real danger.

June 8th. The average man is very like a child; despondent in the time of adversity, and then sanguine and carefree, when the storm has once blown over. Those who some weeks ago were the picture of dejection, as the ravages committed by the French in their villages, have now quite forgotten their misery and are enjoying their high days and holidays, as if we were living in ordinary peaceful days. Lucky for them to have this childlike mind. A French Courier, who came through to-day, told of how he had taken the news of an armistice to the Viceroy in Italy. At this moment, when Austria has such large forces on the frontier, this armistice would seem to point to a peace, but of what kind? Is the blood-thirsty one really tired of bloodshed and longing for peace! Perhaps the whole story is a pack of lies, but true or false, the news is most agitating. Were it not for the thought that a peace might be disadvantageous to Germany, how I should rejoice to think that Leopold was safe, and Ferdinand and Mensdorff no longer obliged to risk their lives.

June 10th. The news of the armistice is only too true. St. Aignan has written to say that it is to last for 2 months. This has come upon us like a thunderbolt from a blue sky, and we are all dreadfully alarmed at the news. To conclude an armistice of 2 months at the moment when Napoleon is cut off from all help by Austria! Peace is sure to follow, and what a peace! It is indeed a sad thing not to be able to rejoice at the thought of peace which is the only thing that could quiet my anxious heart. Ernest has gone to Prague.

July 1st. Ernest writes from Prague, that Metternich is gone to Dresden in order to deliver to Napoleon the last peace offers. The freedom of Germany is the condition and if it is not accepted, then

Austria with her 300,000 troops will go over to the Allies. Ferdinand and Mensdorff are to proceed to Bohemia, in order to join up before the war starts again. The letter has so upset me as well as the imminent departure of my children, that my poor aching head cannot grasp properly all that was said. May God grant that all will turn out for the best!

July 8th. Early this morning Mensdorff brought me a letter from Prague, and in the afternoon there came a 2nd messenger with letters from Ernest and Leopold. A peace congress has been opened, but what will result therefrom? That lies in the hands of Him Who rules the hearts of men. This thought is my comfort, for that Napoleon should willingly give in, is quite inconceivable. The breaking up of the Rhine Confederation is to be the chief condition. Oh! never, never, is he likely to give us back our freedom!

July 9th. Julie has received a letter from the Emperor Alexander, with an invitation to meet him in Bohemia, on the Silesian border. It was a very dear, kind letter. She left this afternoon and will not return here, but go by Prague and Augsburg to Switzerland, there to await the outcome of the storm that may break over our peaceful country.

July 15th. Ernest arrived this morning, bringing, with him a calmer outlook, but little hope of a happy future. The armistice has been prolonged to September 1st, and once more the fate of the people lies in Napoleon's hands. It is for him to decide between peace and war.

August 3rd. Yesterday evening a messenger arrived from Bohemia, and fearing not to be able to get through, Ferdinand and Mensdorff have decided to leave the day after to-morrow. I am quite stunned by this decision, as I had always secretly hoped nothing would come of their plan.

August 5th. They are gone! At 1 o'clock Ferdinand and Mensdorff set forth. It was a hard parting, but I still have a faint hope that there may be peace.

August 10th. To-day unexpectedly the armistice ends. What tragedy will follow the quiet "entre-acte"? From all sides one hears of troops being on the march, which does not hold out much hopes for peace. Our little Contingent has again had to march out although it has already been twice broken up – once in Spain, in 1810 and again last year in Vilna. Where will the poor creatures next find their graves? I could not watch them leave, I pitied them too much.

August 11th. How happy I am to find Sophie and her new-born babe so well. It was christened to-day, receiving the names of Alexander Albert. It made me so sad that good Mensdorff should be absent from the ceremony. The little boy is a healthy little thing, but astonishingly small. I cannot sufficiently thank God for granting Sophie health and strength in a time like this, when she so much needs them.

August 13th. Troops have again been marching through, this morning. They consisted of a medley of French, Dutch and German, all going to face misery and death, with the same reluctance.

August 19th. St Aignan writes that the war is breaking out afresh. Napoleon kept silence up to the last day of the armistice, when his Envoy presented his peace conditions, which were not accepted. Russia and Prussia were tired of the delay, and Austria has declared that she will also be a party to this rejection. May God bless this decision.

August 23rd. A messenger from Eger has brought letters from Ferdinand and Leopold, which have caused us great excitement. I still feel quite shaken. Mensdorff is on the frontier with a patrol corps of Ferdinand's Hussars and Cossacks and may possibly soon come into this neighbourhood. This news has greatly pleased, though at the same time rather agitated Sophie and made her anxious. Ferdinand's appointment as Brigadier of Light Cavalry worries me greatly, for quite apart from the war risks, there is the danger to his health, from the fatigue and exposure, inseparable from outpost work, and I wonder if he will be able to stand it.

August 27th. We have to-day read the Austrian Manifesto. It is impossible to express unpleasant truths in nobler and more tactful fashion. Austria only lays before the world the bare truth, which Napoleon cannot refute. In reading through the Manifesto I am impressed by the way opinions change even in world politics.

Austria will do her best to save Prussia from being annihilated, which is what Napoleon has threatened to do. Half a century ago Austria strove to destroy that state which she is now trying to save, and Frederick the Great intrigued and fought during the whole of his lifetime to undermine Austria's greatness. Little did he dream that both his and Maria Theresa's descendants would form an alliance to check the growing power of France whose warlike activities he had always jeered at.

September 5th. Thank God, very good news has reached us to-day. In the special edition of the Prague newspaper it is said that the French have been totally routed in that lovely country around Töplitz, which they had intended to devastate. Vandamme has been taken prisoner. At first he was only checked by the Russian Guards and a few Austrian Brigades, which included our Coburg Brigade. How my heart rejoiced and how thankful I was that Leopold's name was not amongst the wounded. In Silesia, Blücher has beaten the arrogant enemy and the Crown Prince of Sweden has defeated Marshal Ney near Jüterbock.

September 19th. Thank God, letters have at last come! Both my dear sons have come safely through the sanguinary fighting at the end of last month and the beginning of this. Leopold writes from Töplitz, and Ferdinand from a village in its neighbourhood. The emotion felt on opening these letters has left me quite shaky. Ferdinand fought like a lion with his brave Brigade and greatly helped towards the victory. But he narrowly escaped fatal injury when a bullet hit his breast pocket, the various army orders and a handkerchief, which it contained, stopped the bullet which was already nearly spent. His horse was hit. This narrow escape filled me with horror, and I cannot be sufficiently grateful to God, for having preserved his life. I was not aware that both my sons took part in all the battles since the 25th of August, first in front of Dresden and then in Bohemia.

September 22nd. Daily, fugitives from the dispersed Bavarian Regiments are coming through. They were in the battle near Jüterbock, which resulted in the glorious victory of the Crown Prince of Sweden. To-day the "Chevaux Légers" rode through, but good gracious, on what horses! There has never been such a rout.

September 26th. How happy I am, to have had further letters from Ferdinand and Leopold. On the 13th they were still in good health, for which I am deeply grateful. Ferdinand behaved like a seasoned warrior in these last important events, and Leopold, to whom the "metier" was quite new, did very well. His Emperor gave him and Ferdinand the Cross of the Order of St. George.

September 28th. Early this morning part of Augereau's Corps d'Armée marched through Ketschendorf. It consisted of Hussars, "Chasseurs" and Dragoons. These were followed later by Infantry.

September 29th. More troops continue to arrive. This afternoon we had Maréchal with four Generals and various other officers to lunch. It is undoubtedly true that since the Russian campaign has been lost, Napoleon has forfeited the affection and trust of his officers. This is evident in every word that is spoken. As long as things go well, the French will bear anything and think it good. But as soon as the tide turns, they become discontented and very critical.

September 30th. To-day the last Division consisting mostly of Cavalry, passed through. The Maréchal is still here, but one sees nothing of him, as he is engrossed with business. These passages of troops and the enormous amount of requisitioning are a heavy burden. God preserve us from any fighting or retreating taking place in this peaceful part of the world.

October 7th. A most interesting letter has come from Mensdorff, who has taken part in a very dashing allied Cavalry action in, and near Zeitz. Mercifully he has come safely through.

October 9th. Coburg has returned to-day from Saxony, having seen Mensdorff at Chemnitz, who was, thank God, quite well! He is apparently much beloved and held in high esteem by his comrades-in-arms.

October 21st. I have at this moment received news from Ebersdorf, which has so unnerved me, that I can hardly write. On the 16th and 17th, a fearful battle raged near Leipzig, and what may have been the fate of my sons and what, the result of the Battle?

October 22nd. God be praised, although all three were in the battle, they are safe. A letter from Mensdorff dated the 20th has brought this glad news and I thank God for having answered my prayers. I am almost beside myself with joy. On the 18th they were still fighting, and that day decided the issue. Napoleon was completely defeated. Now we Germans can at last hope that this unnatural Rhine Confederacy into which we were forced by fear and violence will be dissolved. I shall never forget the feelings of degradation and despair which we have endured! Saalfeld and Jena are terrible memories. Drab years followed, and faint hearts almost gave up hope of God's help. But the time was not yet ripe. Now the day of the Lord has some and he has judged! Who can doubt that Providence guided the movement, which brought for the first time all the peoples, of east, north and south together, to resist the destroyer of their freedom and welfare. Russians, Prussians, Swedes, Austrians, and in the south, Spaniards and English joined together in brotherly union against the Power that recognises no right nor law.

October 25th. The Head Quarters of the allied Monarchs are moving to Weimar and Ernest will go there to-morrow. When I hear of the events that have been taking place, I feel as if I were in a dream from which I am afraid to awake. Is it possible that Napoleon's pernicious influence and sway over Germany is coming to an end? It is only Thou, Almighty God, Who couldst break these fetters and give the Allies strength and unity to carry out the deed.

October 26th. How far I was yesterday from expecting the great joy, that has come to me to-day. We had lunched at Ketschendorf and I had only just returned from a walk when someone called out "Prince Leopold is coming." I was so overcome and excited, I could hardly climb the stairs. There stood my beloved boy, and a few paces behind him and officer, whom I did not at first recognise as being the Grand Duke Constantine. It is very nice of him to give me this pleasure.

October 27th. Only to-day can I thoroughly appreciate the joy of having dear Leopold returned to me unharmed, after this fearful campaign. To-day too, I realise how unwell he looks. At midday Ernest arrived. He had met the Emperor Alexander in . . . and ridden all night, which had tired him out.

October 29th. Ernest took the Grand Duke to the Rosenau to-day, which the latter much admired. In the evening there was a Concert. Leopold's health is a great worry to me; every evening he has fever and terrible pains in his head. He complains of being unable to concentrate and of feeling as if he had been stunned. His whole demeanour and character have gained in gravity and decision, since this campaign, but he has grown so deplorably thin and pale, that I cannot look at him without uneasiness. It so often happens that something comes to mar one's joy! Constantine and Leopold have many interesting tales to relate, of the dreadful things they witnessed in the war. The Crown Prince of Sweden, who cannot deny the place of his birth, on the shores of the Garonne, has called the battle of Leipzig, certainly the most awful one for 100 years, "la bataille du monde."

November 4th. Ernest left to-day for Frankfort, where the Head Quarters of the Allies are to be. He will be able to be present at the glorious entry of the allied Monarchs into the ancient city, where the Coronations used to take place. Last year Ernest had unwillingly to witness the proud conqueror in all his glory in Dresden with the Emperor Franz and the King of Prussia in attendance. He had been forced to assist Napoleon in the devastation of the north. Now, only a year after, he, with the same two monarchs, has succeeded in pushing the invincible one back over the Rhine. Who would not recognise the hand of God in this?

November 7th. This morning several hundred Austrian Infantrymen marched in, and it seemed like a dream, to see Austrian troops here once more. Later, there followed "Landwehr." The poor fellows looked as miserable as the weather, and what weather for Infantry! It rains without ceasing. In the afternoon there came the newly created body of Landwehr Dragoons. Barely six weeks have passed since Augereau's Corps d'Armée came through on their way to Saxony, and now it is Austrians and Russians who are here having followed closely on Augereau's heels, pushing him across the Rhine. This rapid change in the situation is almost magic and one hardly dares believe in it!

November 10th. We lunched at Ketschendorf in lovely weather, but our pleasure was rather spoilt by the arrival of a message to Sophie from her husband, bidding her to go to Amorbach, where he would join her. He is stationed at Germersheim on the Rhine. The pleasing prospect of seeing her husband again is somewhat damped by her anxiety at the thought of leaving her children. Mensdorff, in the first days of this month, took part in the battle of Hanau, of which fact we were not at all aware. What a mercy that he has come through so safely!

November 11th. This morning, at four o'clock, Sophie started for Amorbach. I have had a letter from Ernest, from Frankfort, where he has been a spectator of the solemn procession of the Emperors to the Cathedral amidst great public acclamation — the same Cathedral where the Emperor Franz once received the German Imperial Crown. As Ernest was getting out of his carriage, Ferdinand marched past with his Brigade. This meeting was a great joy to them both. Ernest says that Ferdinand was looking very well. I feel so grateful that after all these vicissitudes, the three brothers should have seen each other again and all be alive and well.

November 19th. I have not begun the winter in such a solitary fashion as now since that dreadful year 1806, and if one's thoughts were not so entirely taken up with the present important political events, I should quite give way to depression. But who, in such times, could waste a thought on any small personal troubles or discomforts? All I hear and read of in the papers appears to me still like a dream. The Emperor Alexander must be laughing in his sleeve at the royal bargain hunters who have so quickly turned their coats to the wind now blowing from the north. In 1808, in Erfurt, he saw them crawling before the god of the moment. What an impression must Germany's pitiful and weak-kneed princes have produced on the noble Northern Monarch? When he appeared on the German frontier, he called upon them to work with him to set their country free, instead of which, they let Russia and Prussia fight alone for Germany's freedom and joined with the Oppressor's forces. Only when he was defeated, and Russia, Prussia and Austria had given their blood to ensure victory, did they come forward with zeal for the good cause and strike a blow at the defenceless one!

December 6th. To-day came 476 men of various Russian Cavalry Regiments. Having lost their horses, they have been collecting remounts and a strong detachment of Cuirassiers is accompanying them. These children of the north are handsome, well grown specimens of manhood and their bearing excellent. Some are old and seasoned warriors wearing beards and others vigorous young men. Accustomed as we were to the noisy, talkative French, one is struck by the comparative silence of the Russians in spite of their habit of gesticulation.

December 8th. The sun was shining so enticingly, that, in the afternoon, I drove with Caroline and Hugo to Ketschendorf. Hardly had we got there, when Russian Army wagons came by, to the number of about 150, drawn by miserable looking horses, and driven by men who really looked not unlike bears.

December 10th. This morning we saw the Russians "en parade," marching off again. The stalwart men in full war panoply with all their medals were a fine sight. In the afternoon, in splendid weather, I went to Ketschendorf. Close to the town we met Cossacks on horseback and on foot. I followed them for a while and wondered to myself why these weird creatures did not inspire me with any fear, whilst the French had always inspired me with misgiving. I think it must arise from their insolent, noisy and arrogant manner, which is quite regardless of the feelings of others. The seemingly uncouth Russian is actually both graceful and polite.

December 15th. It is only now that I can think with any composure of a letter I received a few days ago. Sophie and Victoire wrote that they had seen in Frankfort all the Potentates in all their glory. The Emperor Alexander was both affable and friendly. Leopold writes that he and the Grand Duke will march through Amorbach with the "Gardes à Cheval." If Leopold had let me know sooner, I could have gone there and seen him once more. How I regret that I did not long ago make up my mind to go to Amorbach and Frankfort. It is such a unique moment in history when Princes and Soldiers of so many nationalities meet peaceably in one town and such a thing is not likely to happen again! This now useless regret torments me very much and my days have been spent in dreary boredom.

December 20th. The Prussian "Landwehr," which had been sent to us from Erfurt in order that we should feed the men up, has introduced into our midst some sort of low fever. The poor young fellows who have suffered such hardships, only now that the strain has been relaxed, are succumbing to illness. To-day another 100 men have arrived. These serious times press heavily on all of us, but it is only fair that each one should bear their part of the burden. There are still in the country 2000 horses belonging to the Russian Transport and 400 drivers. Cossacks are constantly coming and going and then there is the Russian Commandant with his followers and horses. All this costs a lot and adder to it are the enormous requisitions necessary for the troops engaged in the siege of Erfurt despite the fact that there is a lack of food in the whole surrounding countryside. One must constantly remind oneself that these troops are fighting for our freedoms in order not to resent the fearful burden laid upon us. Meanwhile there remains the hope that with time the benefits of Germany's liberation will come to fruition, and that after the storm, calm and order will reign.

December 30th. The last six months have been dull and dreary, and the year ends in the same way. The gloomy weather, my loneliness, and a bad cough which torments me and prevents my going out, all contribute to my rather depressed state of mind. But I have no time to dwell on this, my thoughts being exclusively occupied with the political events of the day. One only lives for letters and newspapers, and one is constantly in a state of expectation.

December 31st. This important year, in which so much blood has been shed, and which has decided the fate of Germany, indeed of the whole of Europe, is nearly at an end . . . I like the Russian medal, which adorns the breast of every soldier who in the last year fought for his Fatherland. On the one side is represented the eye of God and on the other are engraved the words: "He, not us." Trusting in His strength the noble northern Emperor started the war and God's blessing has followed his army. Will the future rulers of the world ever believe that three mighty Monarchs, indissolubly united, took part in this awful war of nations? It ought to teach them what power there is in unity. It has been a year fought with many a sad day for me. For what a long time, since the early spring, I have been anxious about Leopold, and how I wore myself out with worry all the time before Ferdinand's departure, and how desperate I felt when he and Mensdorff left together! How I trembled for the lives of my sons, exposed to daily dangers! But Thy mighty hand, oh God, has protected them! I should not like to live through such a troubled year again. But it has brought victory to our armies, and freedom to our Country. May we be able at the end of this year to thank Thee, oh God, for the re-establishment of peace!

1 8 1 4

January 1st. The sun has shone brightly on our entry into the new year. Its first rosy streaks pierced through the frosty haze lighting up the trees white with hoar frost, and after a brilliant sunrise we had a glorious day. May it be a good omen for this year, whose first days are still illumined by the fiery torches of war, which please God may be followed by the friendly light of peace. Many a sacrifice and many a burden will this year still cost us, but for the price of peace and freedom, one is ready to face these. How heavily we have had to pay for our fetters, and ought not everyone to be ready and willing to take their share, in the cause of Freedom?

January 2nd. I close, with an earnest prayer for my beloved Ernest, whose birthday it is to-day. May God's blessing and protection be with him throughout the year, with its many anxieties, as it has been in the great dangers of the past one. Had Napoleon been victorious, then Ernest's very existence and whole future would have been hopelessly destroyed.

January 4th. Julie writes to me that she saw Ferdinand, with his troops, enter Berne. When we were peacefully together in Berne, last year, who would ever have dreamt of Ferdinand entering that town with his Brigade. On the 26th December he had moved on with the Corps d'Armée of General Bubna.

January 6th. Sophie has only just put in an appearance, as she has come to fetch the children, whom their Father is very anxious to see, and I shall follow soon, as I cannot any longer bear the loneliness of the "Schloss." The older children were in a tremendous state of excitement at the idea of the journey, but little Hugo did not seem half so pleased when he was told that he, too, was to go to Amorbach.

January 9th. Sophie started off this morning with her children in two carriages, which were quite full up, with the addition of the servants. What a wearisome journey it will be!

January 14th. We were sitting this evening cosily chatting together, when a tall figure came in at the door, which I did not at first recognise – it was Ernest, who had come in a sledge from Frankfort. He will only be able to spend to-morrow with us, but even this short visit is a great pleasure to me.

January 16th. It is thawing hard and poor Ernest will have some difficulty in getting away in his sledge. He has asked his sisters and myself to come this week to see him in Frankfort, and we shall certainly do so.

January 22nd (Frankfort). Yesterday Ernest sent a messenger, begging us to come to-day to Frankfort, as he would not be there much longer. So we set forth this morning at six, and by three o'clock had reached Frankfort. We got out at the big "Schweizersche Haus," on the Zeil, which Ernest had recommended. Mensdorff, who met us on the step, told us that Ernest had not yet come in. We went up the fine marble stairs into the lofty reception rooms, which had only just started to warm, and which were colder than the street. I am afraid I rather grumbled at Ernest inviting us to this inhospitable place. Every little thing we needed had to be fetched from his somewhat distant rooms in the Gallengasse. Meanwhile we waited impatiently for some coffee, still wrapped up in our travelling clothes, hoping to get a little warmer. We tried to entertain ourselves, by watching the busy life in the fine broad street. Ernest came at last, for a few minutes, and then went off with Mensdorff to a dinner to which they had been invited. We had ours late, in our cold, cheerless room. There were piles of wood on the fire, but it did not seem to give out any heat. We went from room to room in a vain search for warmth, and finally, somewhat disgruntled, established ourselves in a small sitting-room.

January 23rd. My children have gone to the Theatre, and I am now enjoying myself by a good fire, which two Coburg soldiers have manged to make for me. They have also lit the stoves. As we were passing over the "Sachsenhauser" Bridge, we saw our little Contingent, which had just arrived. The pleasure the soldiers evinced on seeing us touched me deeply. No one can doubt the sincere devotion of our people. This fine feeling of devotion exists in most German States, where, in spite of it, Napoleon has ever year imposed on them a fresh Ruler, and in some cases succeeded in eradicating the fidelity of the people. The bright sunny winter morning and the military activity in the broad streets, reminded me forcibly of Berlin and of the fateful winter that I spent there seven years ago, seeing under very different circumstances the same sort of scene. At that time Germany's enslavement was beginning, which now, thank God, is over!

January 24th. The Prince Reuss Zu Greiz,[1] and the Russian General Poll, lunched with us, and in the afternoon came Degenfeld, and Count Solms von Laubach, a clever brave man, who has remained true to Germany in the stormy days when many a weak reed bent under the blast. Then also Count Ingelheim, who out of pure patriotism, raised and trained the Frankfort Volunteers, which he will lead into action.

January 26th. Early this morning Princess Ysenburg,[2] with her daughter, and the Princess of Ysenburg-Büdingen, arrived from Offenbach. In the evening we went to the Theatre.

January 29th. We meant to have left to-day but owing to the uncertainty of the approaching visit of the Empress Elisabeth of Russia,[3] we are still kept here.

January 30th. I spent the whole morning answering a disquieting letter from Julie. On the 14th Leopold went to Berne with the Grand Duke and they stayed there some days. Constantine, on meeting his charming wife again, could not refrain from desiring a "rapprochement," and urging it with his usual impulsiveness. Julie amiably declined all his advancers. I cannot blame her for refusing to

---

[1] Henry XIII, Prince Reuss Zu Greiz, at that time Governor-General of Frankfurt.
[2] Charlotte, Princess Ysenburg-Birstein, b. Countess of Erbach-Erbach.
[3] Elisabeth Alexievna, wife of the Emperor Alexander I of Russia, b. Princess of Baden.

resume a life of brilliant misery. After twelve years separation, particularly under existing circumstances, a reunion could never be a happy one. I would give anything to have prevented this meeting taking place.

In the afternoon we paid visits, first to the Reusses and then, to the old Duchess of Nassau,[1] who is always so friendly and pleasant. In the evening we went to the Theatre.

February 1st. At last a courier arrived with the definite news of the Empress's arrival to-morrow. We have therefore not delayed our departure in vain. We lunched with the Prince of Homburg, the Prince of Rudolstadt, Herr von Bethmann, Count Degenfeld, and General Poll. In the afternoon we had a visit from the Dowager Princess of Ysenburg,[2] and later from Prince Frederick of Hesse, and the perpetually shy Hereditary Grand Duke of Hesse-Darmstadt, who came from Reimpenheim.

February 2nd. On a lovely morning I drove out alone to see the new Promenade situated where once stood the ancient walls of the town and I drove right round the now imposing town of Frankfort. Already at four o'clock all the troops were under arms and "en parade." A Squadron of Russian Dragoons were riding out to meet their Empress. Count Degenfeld, Solms von Laubach, and Countess Julie Degenfeld came to us in the afternoon in order to see the arrival of the Empress. At length at seven the guns boomed forth, heralding the arrival, and the Russian Dragoons on their prancing steeds headed the cavalcade and to the accompaniment of cheerful military bands and the boisterous cheers of the Russians and inhabitants of the town, the noble and gracious lady made her entry. Ernest accompanied her to her lodgings and at 8 o'clock he came to tell us that the Empress wished to see us, and that we must dress quickly. This was no easy matter as our maids had gone out to see the illuminations. But we managed it somehow, and hurried across to see the Empress, who received us most cordially, showing unmistakably how pleased she was to see us again. So many memories recurred to me, that I felt quite overcome. The Empress is no longer the young and beautiful Elisabeth I knew in Russia, but she is still the most

[1] Louise, Duchess of Nassau-Ufingen, b. Princess of Waldeck.
[2] Victoria, widow of Prince Wolfgang Ernest II of Ysenburg-Birstein.

noble and graceful woman, who has ever adorned a throne. We spoke much and for a long time, amongst other things of Antoinette, of whom the good Empress is very fond. The Empress's brother, the Grand Duke of Baden and her sister the Hereditary Grand Duchess of Hesse-Darmstadt, a pretty, amiable person, were there. We took our leave before dinner.

February 3rd. All Frankfort was again agog almost at dawn, and the sun shone brightly on an animated scene. Great crowds collected in front of the house where the Empress is staying. I had hoped so much to see her once more alone, but her Chamberlain got up so late, I could obtain no answer from him and then there were whole rows of Princesses waiting to be received. At twelve the Empress left and Sophie and I just went across to bid her farewell. — We attended an evening party which Prince Reuss gave.

February 4th. This morning a battalion of Grenadiers from Berg marched through — fine-looking young men. The Laubachs, Degenfeld, and General Rauch lunched with us, and in the evening, all excepting myself went to a Concert.

February 5th. This morning I drove to Offenbach to visit my oldest friend, the Dowager Princess Ysenburg, who has a very nice house, in that pleasant little town. In the evening we went to the Theatre. As soon as we got home, a courier arrived with the news of Blücher's success in beating the French at Troyes.

February 6th. To-morrow we shall be leaving Frankfort. Much as I enjoy seeing Ernest and Mensdorff, I shall be very glad to be leaving. The gentlemen are overwhelmed with unpleasant business, no one looks cheerful, and the inhabitants are irritated by the billeting arrangements which impose on them a tremendous burden. The general feeling of discontent adds to the discomfort of this somewhat grand and uncomfortable hotel.

February 7th (Amorbach). We left Frankfort this morning after nine, and got here by four in the afternoon. A thorough thaw has set in and fitful gleams of sunshine lit up the countryside between snow storms. I feel comfortable and warm in my cosy room and appreciate the quiet after the busy days at Frankfort and the discomforts of that wretchedly cold hotel. I ought never to travel again in winter, it no longer agrees with me.

February 10th. Jews coming from Frankfort brought the news of a glorious victory at Brienne. On the very day Elisabeth came here, her brave people were fighting in France, and the Emperor himself was facing danger! How lucky it is for us poor mortals that we are not all endowed with second sight!

February 11th. The papers have confirmed the news of the glorious victory. Thank God, that the Russian "Gardes à Cheval" did not take part in it, neither did Ferdinand, for it was a very dearly bought victory. Naturally he is very vexed at being condemned to blockade Besançon, whilst others were earning distinction and will take part in the glorious entry into "la capitale du monde," I can quite understand his feelings; but all the same I am deeply grateful that he was not exposed to the great dangers of those days.

February 13th. To-day we have thanked God with our whole hearts and with national solemnity for the victories achieved, by the noble men who fought for our freedom. It is to be hoped that the brilliant victories of Brienne and La Rotière will soon assure us Peace, that peace of which the whole of Europe stands so sorely in need.

February 21st. Ferdinand writes to me on the 6th that he is still at Besançon, where he sits and shivers, wearied to death and intensely bored by this prolonged blockade. He also minds very much not having been able to take part in the fighting for Paris. I am afraid I cannot participate in this regret, for I am very thankful that he was not exposed to the great dangers there. He has already twice bombarded and set poor Besançon on fire.

March 8th. To-day there has been further very heartening news of victories. The French have been completely surrounded by Blücher and Wintzingerode and thoroughly beaten. Thank God for this! Though I cannot rejoice unreservedly until I have heard from Leopold.

March 10th. At last a letter has come from Leopold, from Brunet near Troyes. He had not yet taken part in any engagement, but was tired to death by the constant long marches, and the bivouacking in the cold. What health can withstand the present mode of carrying on warfare?

March 15th. Julie has sent me a copy of a letter she has received from Ferdinand which makes me intensely uneasy. The small Corps d'Armée of Louis Lichtenstein to which Ferdinand's brigade is attached, is constantly engaged in actions which cost heavy losses and they are threatened by Marshal Augereau's army from Lyons. They are lost if he strikes at them with his far larger army.

March 19th. The Austrian Emperor and the King of Prussia were already deliberating some sort of patched-up peace, the one in order to spare his daughter, the other from weariness at the long and sanguinary war, but the Emperor Alexander remained adamant and Napoleon, blinded by some successes, refused to consider such a peace. On the 10th the Allies were again victorious, and made him pay dearly for his refusal. The besiegers of Besançon have now also been reinforced, which is satisfactory.

March 31st. For some time my little pet, Alfred, has not been so bright, and he has been so long over his teething, that I have been worrying about him wondering if he might have picked up some germ, he is so altered and so quiet.

April 3rd. This evening news came from Frankfort of further victories gained on the one side by Schwarzenberg and Wrede, and in the centre of France by Wellington. May God continue to bless our armies and give us peace, which we so urgently need. But in spite of all these successes, I am very uneasy about Leopold.

April 5th. Thank God, I have got news of Ferdinand. Julie writes on the 30th that Ferdinand's Corps has been moved from Besançon to hold up the enemy until the arrival of Field-Marshal Bianchi who defeated the latter, and on the 27th St. Etienne, near Lyons, where there is an important Munition Factory, was taken. How glad I am once again to get some definite news of Ferdinand. Probably he may be exposed to greater danger there than at Besançon, but he is much happier and has more opportunities of distinguishing himself, which means so much to him.

April 8th (Good Friday). This peaceful and holy day ends with wild rumours, and overwhelming manifestations of joy. At seven this evening a courier brought the official news of the capitulation of Paris and that the Emperor of Russia and King of Prussia, at the head of their Guards, had entered the ci-devant capital of the world. With an enthusiasm that can never be equalled we heard the news of this great event. Leiningen ordered the Church bells to be rung immediately and their beautiful deep tones sounded impressively in the calm night. One could hear from the Roman Catholic church the soft sounds of Good Friday's closing Service, and their bells also started to ring as soon as this ended. An unheard-of thing on Good Friday! The air reverberated with cheers from the populace and the constant firing of guns, which echoes in the hills. The dreaded, mighty Conqueror has brought things to such a pass, that foreign armies are now entering Paris. How often he might have made peace, but moderation was unknown to him and he was so accustomed to dictate his will, that he preferred staking everything on a gamble, rather than yield to necessity. I wonder what the results of the fall of Paris will be for him?

April 10th. To-day Sophie went with Hugo to Oppenheim, to be present at the solemn Te Deum for the Troops. In the afternoon here, there was a big dinner. One is not likely to get much sleep, and I pity the poor children in all this din, particularly little Alfred, who screams at every sound of a gun.

April 15th (Heidelberg). I little thought yesterday that I should be spending the night to-day at Heidelberg. In the night, at ten o'clock, a courier came from Julie from Bruchsal, letting me know she expected to be at Heidelberg on the 14th and would like to spend the 15th with me. There was no time to be lost, and half asleep, I decided to go and made hurried preparations. I managed to get away by 4.30. As we got into the picturesque valley of the Neckar, there were lovely signs of spring and many leaves already out. In the gardens the fruit trees were showing blossoms and right in the valley it was very hot. We reached Heidelberg at 5 and Julie was overjoyed at seeing me.

April 16th (Mannheim). Julie accompanied me as far as Schwetzingen, where we lunched after having visited the Gardens. Spring is far more advanced here than in the Odenwald.

Schwetzingen was full of flowers and flowering shrubs. We parted reluctantly at about 4 o'clock. I had only an hour's journey before me, but Julie had 8, to get back to Bruchsal! I was welcomed very heartily by my sister and her family. They have a charming house on the "Paradeplatz," but there is not sufficient room to take me in, so I am lodging at the so-called Palais. I hear that Ernest, who is expected to-morrow, for the celebrations in commemoration of the taking of Paris, will also stay here.

April 17th (in the morning). I have been watching from the balcony in front of the reception rooms of the Palace, half Mannheim proceeding to church for the Te Deum. Their rejoicings seemed to me rather half-hearted, and as feeble as the sounds of the gun salvoes, which were hardly audible. This was probably due to their sympathy with Stephanie over Napoleon's downfall.

April 18th (in the morning). I could not manage yesterday to write any more. At one o'clock, my brother-in-law fetched me, and I found at his house the chief notabilities of the town whom he had invited to luncheon. In the evening we went to a beautifully decorated Theatre, where a play called "Hermann or the Deliverance of Germany," was given. Ernest came in towards the end, and was received with clapping of hands, to which, thank goodness, he is much too sensible, to attach any great importance. It was meant only for the General in Command of the 5th Army Corps, stationed near by, whose influence can help or injure these of the Mannheim people who have properties on the Rhine. From the theatre we went at 10 to a Ball, which was very pretty.

In the evening. Ernest lunched to-day with the Köstritzes[1] before going to Bruchsal to see Julie, and then pay his respect to the Empress.

April 22nd (Oppenheim). I left Mannheim this morning, at 7, and took leave with much regret of my brother-in-law. For I don't know when I shall see him again. My sister and Carrie Reuss-Köstritz[1] accompanied me as far as Oggersheim. It gave me quite a strange feeling, after twenty years, to find myself again in the district of the Upper Rhine, which is much altered. We got here at about 2. Oppen-

[1] Brother-in-law and niece of the Duchess.

heim is an unusual and rather large town built on the side of a hill. In the distance one can see Worms and Darmstadt and beyond them the "Bergstrasse." After dinner, a courier came from Amorbach with very disturbing news. Alfred is again very unwell and suffering from great exhaustion. Sophie is hurrying there early to-morrow morning.

In the evening. We lunched in Bodenheim, where various French Generals had assembled to confer together but not much has resulted from this meeting. It was, to decide what they might take away from Mayence, as against what they wanted to take away! They are deeply pained by the humiliation of their position and the pitiful ending to the great Napoleonic adventure.

April 24th. Mensdorff has also gone to Amorbach this morning, and I am terribly anxious about the news a courier is to bring me to-morrow.

April 25th. Alas! the messenger has come with the news that my poor little pet is dying. Sophie wrote the following: "You will never see your little darling again, the feeble little lamp is only just flickering between life and death."

April 29th. Alfred is dead! The lovely little blossom has withered and the dear sweet child has gone to join his brothers, amongst the angels. Oh God, in cutting short a young life, Thou dost inflict on us the heaviest of all sorrows! But we know that Thy ways are best and Thy reasons always good!

In the evening. This morning the Saxon banner has crossed the Rhine. Ernest with his "Etat-Major", A.D.C.s etc., rode out to meet the troops, who acclaimed him as they filed past. I hope that soon his military role will be ended as Mayence is being given over. Life in such Head Quarters has no doubt a certain glamour and the busy active life is naturally entertaining. The command being in the hands of a bad man, might, however, as one can easily understand, lead to abuses.

May 1st. I wanted to leave to-morrow for I have not a moment's peace of mind away from my poor Sophie, in her great distress. But as the handing over of Mayence is already to take place on the 4th, I have allowed myself to be persuaded to delay my departure in order to be present at so remarkable an event, which means so much for Germany.

May 4th (Mayence). Quite unexpectedly I am sitting here, in this old town of Mayence, thoroughly exhausted, after a most fatiguing day. Thank goodness that this powerful fortress, the siege of whose walls would have caused rivers of blood to flow, has been ceded to the Allies without a shot being fired. The loss of Mayence has been a terrible blow to the French, who seem quite to forget that it is a German town. In the finest streets of the rambling old city we watched the entry of the troops. It was an imposing sight to see that mighty army advancing, Regiment after Regiment, I should say to the amount of about 30,000 men. What a mercy that these fine troops have been saved and given back to their Fatherland after so many losing their lives. Towards the end of the procession we drove on to the German "Ordenshaus" which has been the Palais Imperial, and which has now been placed at Ernest's disposal. It is a fine large building, overlooking the Rhine. Now I am sitting in what was Marie-Louise's bedroom. What tears may the poor woman not have shed in this room and what terrors must she have gone through last year when Napoleon left her here, to go and make war on her Father!

May 5th. I am leaving to-morrow and in a few days Ernest and Mensdorff are going to Paris.

May 6th (Amorbach). I end this day thinking with a heavy heart of the dear little departed one, and much more upset by the sight of Sophie's intense grief, than by the fatigue of the journey. The sight of the other children without their darling brother, makes me dreadfully sad.

May 7th. Sophie left early this morning for Mayence, I order to see her husband once more, before he goes to Paris. I am quite glad of this little "déplacement", as I hope it may prove a slight distraction to her thoughts, and do her good.

May 24th. I had a letter to-day from Ernest from Paris, written in rather a gloomy and disheartened frame of mind. The promising prospects of the peace are bearing bitter fruit and Germany, after her hard sacrifices and the great events on which so much was staked, does not seem likely to be any the happier. It is as if there were evil forces in Paris, which turn all noble endeavours into tricks for selfish ends.

June 4th. The Löwensteins with visitors came to tea. The two officers who have come from Paris told us that the French are more arrogant than ever and cannot brook having been beaten, going to far as to brag loudly that in a year's time they would reconquer all they had lost!

June 8th. This morning I received a courier from Ernest, who has got back to Mayence. Leopold has gone with the Russian Emperor to London. He will never undertake a more interesting journey, and I hope to welcome him in Coburg on his return. Ernest is coming to Frankfort with the Grand Duke Constantine and I shall also be going there the day after to-morrow.

June 9th. To-morrow quite early, I shall be starting for Frankfort, carrying away with me grateful memories of pleasant peaceful days spent here. For years I have not seen Leiningen in such a friendly mood, showing that my visit has given him much pleasure and I certainly have never found a winter pass by so quickly. I am positively startled when looking at the green trees, to realise that I have been here since January, when I only intended to stay 6 weeks!

June 10th (Frankfort). It was a lovely morning for setting forth on my journey and the country looked beautiful in the bright sunshine. I arrived this evening at 9 and to my great consternation find that the Grand Duke has already left and that he not only enquired for me, but had all the hotels in Frankfort ransacked in order to try to find me. He was to get to Weimar this evening. Leiningen and Victoire also meant to come here, and I waited for them the whole afternoon. At last they arrived and we had tea together, being joined by Prince Reuss, Count Solms von Laubach and a Herr von Tischler who had a great deal of news to give us from Paris, but nothing very pleasant.

June 11th (Mayence). After rather a disturbed night owing to heavy traffic passing by uninterruptedly till dawn, I breakfasted with Victoire before starting for Mayence at 9. I was very sorry to take leave of her and her husband. We got to Mayence at 2, and were heartily welcomed by Ernest, who I thought looked very unwell. He has returned from Paris with a swollen face and toothache.

June 12th. One would have expected to see nothing but cheerful faces, now there is peace, however, this is anything but the case. People seem to be oppressed by some dreadful fear of possible coming events. But vanity taken for magnanimity, weakness, and levity have spoilt the peace and have only laid the seeds for further trouble. But the French have succeeded in wriggling out of the grip of the scissors, which were intended to clip their wings, and yet they are not satisfied with the unwise leniency shown them. They still consider themselves to be the first people of the world, boast that they have never been beaten and insist that the Allied Powers will have to give back what they have taken, and then a terrible retribution awaits them! Ernest will be leaving here in a few days, as his Corps d'Armée is going to be disbanded, and the Austrians and Prussians are going to occupy Mayence. At first the Bavarians wanted to do this and it is evident that none want to give way to the other. Oh perverse humanity, that neither the cross of adversity nor peace and happiness, seem to improve!

June 15th (Ketschendorf). I am still dreadfully tired by my hurried journey and can hardly move. On the 13th I breakfasted with Ernest before leaving Mayence at about 8. I only changed horses at Frankfort and drove on past Seligenstadt to Aschaffenburg, which I had not seen for a long time and which has been much beautified. The sun was going down as we came to the renowned Spessart country, which it lit up with its golden rays, and in the valleys dusk was already falling. The woods became very quiet and shrouded in mystery, and the cool night air was perfumed with the scents of fresh green leaves. It must have been about 11 when we stopped at the rather notorious post house of Rohrbrunnen. This lonely house in the midst of the dark forest, involuntarily made one think of past days of robbery and violence. The dawn was breaking as we left the Spessart and came to Rohrbrunnen. Numbers of larks were singing their morning song above the corn fields. At 5 we passed through Würzburg without stopping to breakfast, but when we reached Neuses-am-Sand, hunger compelled us to ask for a cup of coffee and some bread and butter. Bamberg, which we passed at 4, was crowded with Russians, and war equipment of every kind. The road and weather were equally good, and a lovely evening closed a most glorious summer's day. We reached here at 11, thoroughly tired out and nearly all the inhabitants of the town had already retired for the night, excepting Hohenbaum, who with his little lantern came out of the empty Ehrenburg to see what carriage was passing, and recognising us, gave us a warm welcome. But we did not delay and came straight on here.

June 20th. To-day our Volunteer Jäger and Landwehr, all garlanded with greenery, have made a formal entry into the town. The joy of the good peasantry at seeing their poor boys, many of whom had been mere children when they left, return safe and sound and grown into men, was unbounded, and I felt one with them. Even though the peace terms have not come up to our expectations of what we considered we were entitled to after such a glorious ending to the war, many a heart that had trembled for its dear ones is now happy and praising God.

June 25th (Ketschendorf). I came this afternoon to Ketschendorf to await Ernest's arrival. After tea I heard my name being called from outside. It was a young Saxon officer of Hussars, who was just dismounting from his horse, and had come to announce the arrival of Ernest. Soon the latter, with Hardenbrock, arrived, and I was very thankful to see him restored to his usual health. When they left Amorbach, Leiningen was slightly better.

June 29th. This afternoon, Mensdorff, Sophie, and the dear boys arrived, bringing thus a little life again into the house, but how painfully I miss afresh my sweet little pet.

July 2nd. At 11, volunteer Saxon troops came through Ketschendorf, and Ernest, Uncle, Mensdorff, and all the officers rode out to meet them. Our fine Battalion also came with them. They drew up on the "Schlossplatz" to be inspected by Ernest, and it was a stirring sight. Many officers came to dinner. A Saxon Captain, lately returned from London, was quite delighted with the reception given by the English people, which was not only for the Monarchs, but also for each individual, who had fought in the great struggle, all being treated with the same distinction.

July 3rd. To-day was celebrated in the old "Stadt-Kirche" the solemn Te Deum for the cessation of the war. Good old Uncle, who has taken part in so many peace celebrations, the Saxon General, the Hereditary Prince of Hildburghausen, and the Russian officers walked in the procession to the church with Ernest at the head of the troops. The excellent Hoffländer delivered a dull address. I think he must have been rendered nervous by the presence of so many distinguished and learned men amongst the simple soldiers, for he said nothing at all worthy of this great occasion. Many a serious thought passed through my mind of present and past important times, and I tried to thank God for His leniency to us. The music was very impressive and fine.

July 4th. Early this morning the Saxon troops marched away again. May God's blessing go with them! Seldom could a Corps of 3000 men be gathered together again, in whose different ranks there are so many distinguished men. In Mayence three Sharpshooters took leave of the Corps, the one to go as Professor to Heidelberg, the other to Stuttgart, the third remaining at Mayence as a teacher.

The same evening. I have had a great joy. Ferdinand arrived this afternoon looking very well and none the worse for all the dangers he has been exposed to.

July 5th. This afternoon there came a courier from Amorbach. I was so alarmed that I hardly dared to open the letter, for I suspected what its contents would be. The Doctors had thought all danger was past when serious lung trouble supervened, and the poor sufferer whose weakened condition prevented his rallying, passed peacefully away yesterday morning. This news has much upset me. How little did I suspect when I took leave of good Leiningen at Frankfort, that it was the last time I should see him on earth! For dear Victoire and her children his death is naturally a great grief, but not a calamity. His many good qualities were somewhat spoilt by his hasty temper and obstinacy which made him enemies. Now all that is past, and my good gentle daughter and her fatherless children, may perhaps more readily obtain the protection and help they could not get before. May God give peace to the poor troubled man, who had been so depressed and so much resented the downfall of his family, so cruelly brought about by Napoleon. The last years of poor Leiningen's life had been a constant fight between inimical feelings and a restless striving to get back his independence — a thing impossible to obtain any more. When I went to Amorbach last winter I found him much altered and his spirit broken. He was more mild and friendly than I had seen him for years, but he seemed very weary both in mind and body. Seldom did is sparkling spontaneity of former years break out, which had made intercourse with him so attractive. He did, however, occasionally let fall some caustic remark about the world's events. I was convinced he would not have to endure life much longer, though I little thought his end was so near. I shall always treasure a pleasant memory of his friendliness during the last months of his life.[1]

July 6th. Sophie went off early this morning to Amorbach, to be of some help and comfort to her sister, in these sad days.

July 10th. A letter from Victoire, very broken by the loss of her husband, has made me very sad, for I realise that my poor child is going to be severely tried by the difficult circumstances which face her. May God help her to make some order out of chaos, so that she may finally regain happier conditions.

July 21st. I breakfasted with Ferdinand in his garden and remained the whole day in the town. Ernest came to tea. He and Ferdinand leave to-night for Frankfort and then, Amorbach.

July 22nd. On a very rainy evening, Sophie, her husband and children arrived in time for tea, and now I am occupying myself in looking through my Diary of the beginning of last year. What painful memories it awakes of all my anxiety for my sons in those terrible times and it arouses a sense of gratitude that they are over.

August 4rd. To-day is the first birthday of pretty black eyed little Alexander. May God bless the dear child!

August 10th. Ernest and Mensdorff returned last night from Amorbach and breakfasted here with me. We sat some time talking and then we all drove into the town for luncheon.

---

[1] Emich Carl, Prince of Leiningen, Victoire's husband, died on July 4.

August 11th. At 9 this morning Leopold arrived, Ferdinand breakfasted here, and Ernest came over from the Rosenau. With what joy I welcomed the dear boy, who is looking well, and how unspeakably happy and thankful I am to have my three sons together again after the dreadful experiences of the war. My heart is full of what might have happened which God has so mercifully averted, by sparing them and my son-in-law.

August 13th. I cannot help regretting that one does not sufficiently appreciate the blessings of peace. An uncomfortable feeling of fear as to what its results may be for Germany, seems to cloud over all real happiness. The German has accustomed himself to disquietude and anxiety, and cannot yet quite grasp his present condition of security. All the ugly passions, such as envy, jealousy, greed, and egotism, which the common fear kept dormant, have now, with the assurance of peace, come to the surface. The great deeds ended with the war, heroism has not outlasted the danger, and no one seems any longer to give a thought to the welfare and happiness of the people, their rights, and their freedom. Those who have a higher ideal for what is great and good look with disgust on the present wave of materialism which has followed on the noble outbursts of enthusiasm of the first days of the peace.

August 22nd. Leopold has just returned quite dead-tired from shooting. It gives me great pleasure that he is living here again just as in the days of his early youth! and inhabits with pleasure the same little rooms he used to occupy.

September 7th. A week more, and then my sons will be leaving. We have had such a delightful, though far too short, time together! Leopold has been here hardly four weeks, and goodness knows when I shall see him again. In a few months, he will be leaving for the north, and when will he return to his family from that distant land? Will all three brothers ever come together again as now? Each year conditions change, and rarely for the better. The happy, heedless time together, of their early youth, is long past. Politics and public business, all create anxieties for the future and obliterate the memories of the old happy days.

September 10th. I am counting with sorrow the few more days till my dear ones leave me. In the evening we talked of a great deal of present-day events, — of the selfishness, self interest, levity, foolishness and all the many human failings that are spoiling the hard work of reconstruction. It seems as if only unimportant people were anxious for good to prevail, whereas those who could further it, are only thinking of their own advantage.

September 17th. Ernest is staying one day longer, but all these last ones, with their preparations for the departure, depress me inexpressibly. After the lapse of some months, I am likely to see Ernest again, Ferdinand who is going to Bohemia, I hope, some time in the coming year, but Leopold I cannot think when! He is remaining on a day or two longer, for which I am truly grateful.

September 18th. Ernest and Ferdinand left at five this morning. God grant that Ernest may obtain at the Congress of Vienna what he so ardently desires and may present his request wisely.

September 24th. I close this last day Leopold is spending with us, sorrowfully and tired out. It has been a lovely day and I regretted having to go into the town. The heat of the rooms and the many people who came to wish Leopold goodbye, contributed to give me a very bad headache.

September 25th. God go with him, the dear kind heart, who shows so much affection for his mother, and may He grant him, what will be for his good and his happiness.

October 18th. I am quite tired and agitated by all the memories evoked by the first anniversary of the Battle of Leipzig which decided the fate of the whole of Germany and that of Europe as well. What an amount of lives it cost, to achieve this great victory! This eventful day has been duly celebrated here, as elsewhere. At nightfall, the first salute was fired from the Fortress and in the town the bells were rung. A choir, surrounded by burghers with lighted torches, sang "Eine feste Burg ist unser Gott," on the Market Place. It was a warm evening, and at dusk the flames of bonfires on all the hills lit up the cloudless sky. It was quite an impressive sight to see the whole countryside illuminated as if by one belt of fire.

October 19th. What an awakening! With the first rays of the sun came a salute from the guns, and in the courtyard a Band played the beautiful hymn "Now thank we all our God." I can truly join in this gratitude to the Almighty, more especially as I have been granted the privilege of my sons lives being spared, so that nothing need impair the happiness of the day; the disgrace of Germany is now wiped out for ever!

November 9th. Last night in heavy rain Julie arrived, looking very well, young and pretty. I am so happy to have her with me.

November 30th. Ferdinand has written from Vienna, in such a gloomy disconnected frame of mind, that I am seized with a fear as to the outcome of this wretched Congress which appears to me like Pandora's box which once opened releases so many passions that cannot be controlled. All the beautiful assurances that preceded it may very likely never be fulfilled.

December 16th. God's blessing on this day, my dearest Leopold's twenty-fourth birthday, which I had so much hoped he would have been able to spend with me. May his future be as happy a one as his early youth was. He will have now to face more serious and important undertakings, and I say to myself with a heavy heart, that perhaps never again will he spend this day with us. May God protect him on his way to a northern country, which is not usually very friendly to foreigners, and give him wisdom and courage to hold his own and not allow himself to be influenced by heartless people, who may attempt to turn him from the right path.

December 31st. This eventful year has now also come to a close. The Tyrant has been thrown from his pedestal, and peace reigns from the North to the Mediterranean. And yet I, in common with, I am sure, most thinking Germans, cannot end it with quite the same enthusiasm as the previous one. Greatly and gloriously did the war end at Mont-Martre, but with the calm of peace, alas, all the ugly passions of men have reappeared and that which even Napoleon could not take from us — hope — is now dwindling. But the same God still reigns, and in His might and wisdom, I put my trust, and thus go forward to meet the unknown, with calm faith!

1815

January 19th. Never do I feel the love of my children so deeply as on my birthday, when they take such pains to give me pleasure. I am most grateful for each happy moment of the day. My sister's presence added to this. I was awakened by some very nice music. Julie invited us to a "déjeuner" at 10, and hardly had we sat down, than we heard sounds of approaching music and there appeared a procession of miniature couples, of various nationalities, each bearing gifts. Hugo and Alphonse took part, representing Cossacks. It would be impossible to see a prettier collection of children, playing their parts so seriously and with so much decorum. This party broke up at 12, but was followed, later on, by further celebrations, all charmingly thought out.

January 25th. To-day was little Alphonse's fifth birthday, in honour of which there was a children's dance. Many of the little guests were the same as attended my birthday, and they made a very happy evening of it.

January 26th. Our dear old Uncle's[1] health is causing us a good deal of anxiety. He can neither eat nor sleep because of the pain in his leg which has been troublesome for some time and he has a good deal of fever. How can one expect an old man of 77 to stand this for long?

February 4th. Ferdinand has told me to-day of his happy and brilliant matrimonial prospects. He has lost his heart to the charming daughter of Count Cohary. His affection is returned, and he is fortunate to have captivated such an heiress, who according to Ernest's letter, is as good as she is pretty. This unexpected news has greatly agitated me. God seems always to have watched specially

[1] Prince Josias of Saxe-Coburg-Saalfeld.

over my dear Ferdinand. He returned from the war so hurt and discouraged, with the feeling of being unwanted, and having no object in life. He entered the war with such keenness and enthusiasm, only to return disillusioned. I was beginning to fear he would become quite hypochondriacal, realising that, unknown to himself, he was longing for a life of more activity and responsibility. Thou hast now, oh God, solved all his troubles and granted him this great happiness!

February 6th. Dear old Uncle is getting daily weaker. His strong constitution enabled him to make a gallant fight, but at his advanced age, it is impossible for his strength to hold out much longer.

February 18th. Late last night Mensdorff was summoned to Uncle's bedside, he had relapsed into a state of coma. It would seem that there is no longer any hope of preserving that life so precious to all. Beloved and respected he was like an old patriarch amongst us and the last survivor of his generation. He took such a pride in my sons and Ferdinand's happy prospects had even now given him much pleasure. He had still so many interests in this world that he leaves it unwillingly.

February 25th. What we have been dreading for weeks has happened to-day. Our dear Uncle is dying, and I cannot bear to think of his last struggle for life. God make it easy for him and may His angels help him through the everlasting gates!

February 26th. This morning at 3 Uncle passed away painlessly without having recovered consciousness. I cannot say how deeply grieved I am. His character was such a truly noble one and so full of real sympathy. Few people play their part in life so well up to the very end, as he did, without any lapse or weakness. In his youth he was a good son and enjoyed to the full a happy guileless life. Later on, he became a very distinguished soldier and a good leader, the pride of his whole family, who probably without him would never have taken such a prominent place in the annals of the times. In his old age he was a calm and happy man and kind to everyone. Till the last months of his long life he had never been ill, therefore pain, to which he was unaccustomed, struck him harder than other people, but his brain remained clear and bright until the last.

March 2nd. The people of Coburg to-day followed our beloved Uncle with genuine sorrow to his grave. They were double proud of him as a distinguished military leader and the son of their deeply revered Duke Francis Josias. The grief of Uncle's own people was heartrending to behold. They had been so long with him, the latest comer 17 years and the oldest, his steward, 53 years!

March 14th. What startling news to-day's papers contain; Napoleon has escaped from Elba! It is inconceivable that such a dangerous man, should not have been more carefully guarded. I have been frightened to death by this news and according to a letter from Leopold, the Sovereigns in Vienna not less so. I have so often before agitated myself unnecessarily, that I will not now give myself over to gloomy forebodings.

March 16th. I was awakened this morning at 6, by someone creeping up to my bed. It was Mensdorff, who came to tell me, in great excitement, that Sophie had most happily and easily given birth to her fourth son. How I thank God for this great mercy!

March 25th. Every day more troubled news is coming from France. Ernest has written to Mensdorff to send a courier to the Corps d'Armée, and to be prepared to receive his marching orders. These may come in a very few days and poor Sophie has not yet recovered.

March 27th (Easter Monday). This afternoon the dear little baby was christened, receiving the names of Leo Emanuel. May God bless him!

March 28th. It is good Ferdinand's birthday, which he is spending with the sweet girl who is to become his wife, only too soon to be torn from her, and to have again to face the horrors of war. May God preserve him and in due time may he return to his family unharmed!

May 1st. I went rather early to Ketschendorf and had a solitary luncheon on the balcony where I had been sitting the whole morning. A thunderstorm drove me in, and I sat by the window, from which I soon saw a carriage approaching. Ferdinand stepped out of it, but my great joy at seeing him was somewhat spoilt when he told me he could only be here for a few days, having to rejoin his Brigade. His poor little Fiancée wrote me such an affectionate and piteous letter.

This trying parting is probably the first real sorrow she has had in her young life.

May 9th. I could not any longer endure the town in this heavenly weather and have to-day moved into my summer quarters here. I have spent the whole morning in Ferdinand's garden where we had breakfast together. One could hear the nightingales in the shrubbery and overhead the larks, soaring up into the blue sky.

May 15th. Ferdinand left this morning and I took leave of him with a heavy heart. May God protect him as He has done hitherto, and may the dear boy be brought back safely to the arms of his Fiancée.

May 23rd. Ferdinand has written to say that he is posted to the "Corps" of Prince Hohenzollern and again, alas, to the "avant garde"! This worries me, on account of his being exposed to much greater fatigues and because his health is still far from being completely restored.

June 1st. Ernest has just arrived at half-past 10 and stopped for a few moments. He is looking very well.

June 14th. Ferdinand writes to me from Heilbronn. He has received the Cross of the Order of St. Theresa, in recognition of his conduct near Kulm. Field-Marshal Schwarzenberg decorated him in the presence of the Monarchs, the entire Head Quarters Staff and in front of the 4th Cavalry Regiment. This great distinction, which he was pleasantly conscious of having well earned, gave him much pleasure.

June 23rd (Coburg). On a very stormy wet morning, I went into the town. We were all together, taking tea with Julie when a post-chaise laden with luggage drew up at the Schloss. Everyone shouted out "Leopold"! and I could hardly breathe for excitement. A moment like that makes up for many a dreary hour. Evidently he was also very pleased at being with us again.

June 26th. Mensdorff leaves to-night for Head Quarters and hopes to get back in about a week or ten days. I ought to be very pleased at the news of a victory in the Netherlands, but it was such a hard fought battle[1] and cost the Allies so many lives, it is rumoured, as many as 20,000 men, that it is impossible to rejoice whole-heartedly, when one thinks of all this carnage that took place on the 15th, 16th and 17th. Wellington has again proved his capacity as a General and old Blücher his valour. The English and Germans fought like lions and Napoleon who himself led his armies was completely beaten. This brilliant victory is a fine beginning to the campaign but I can think of nothing else excepting that war has started again, and that already thousands have perished. The Duke of Bunswick[2] is amongst the fallen and I have been much upset by his death, and so has Ernest, who only saw him a short time ago in Vienna. Poor unlucky man, hardly had he resumed possession of his Duchy, than he is killed on the field on honour, like many another noble Guelf. It is awful to think that my three sons are again taking part in this war.

June 29th. To-day in lovely weather we settled to go to the Rosenau, and arrived just at the same time as an Austrian Officer who came from Head Quarters and will remain with Ernest. Everything is moving very quickly and it is hoped that the battle won at Belle-Alliance [Waterloo] will have far-reaching results. God grant that it may soon end the war.

July 7th. I am waiting for Leopold with a heavy heart, he is coming to supper, before wishing me goodbye. To-night he goes off to join the Imperial Head Quarters, but I doubt if he will catch them up, before they have advanced a good way into France., It is sad for me to see him go, although he is not likely to be exposed to much danger, but one can never tell what may happen before we meet again. I shall miss him very much his calm, cheerful and pleasant companionship. Good, amiable and clever, he does deserve a happy future. All my prayers accompany him.

July 12th. This morning all the men of the Ducal Saxon Regiment assembled here, preparatory to marching off to-morrow. All the officers, from Meiningen, Hildburghausen, as well as from here were entertained to luncheon in the Schloss. The Regiment looked in

[1] The Battle of Waterloo, fought on the 18th.
[2] Frederick William, Duke of Brunswick.

splendid condition, the men in the highest of spirits. It is to be hoped that all will be over by the time they get to France. Wellington and Blücher entered Paris on the 6th. For the 2nd time within 15 months that proud people has to bear this painful humiliation, which it has brought on himself.

July 19th. The Allied Kings have for the second time made their entry as victors into the "Capitale du Monde," and Louis the XVIII[1] has been restored to his Throne amidst the joyous acclamations of the good people of Paris! What a pitifully fickle nation! If true greatness is only produced by misfortune, then during these last years the French have forfeited all claims to such greatness.

July 25th. Good Ernest is gone, and with him all the life and brightness of the house. I am not anxious about him, as I was about Ferdinand, when he left, but I nevertheless feel sad and depressed at the emptiness and silence around me.

August 3rd. Ernest writes that he has marched with the Saxons to Dijon. I am not very pleased about this, as I had hoped he would remain in Alsace. He may meet with many unpleasant experiences in that starved, disordered part of the world.

August 8th. Ernest sent me a few lines by a Saxon Jäger, to tell me that his plans are again changed and that he is going to Colmar in Alsace to be under the orders of the Archduke John.

August 10th. It is a sad peculiarity of our times, that even good people's actions are so often inspired by self-interest. The right course must always be the one in which usefulness and honour are combined. Soon we shall have to look to the heroes of bygone days, and in romances, for the noble, great-hearted men who place their principles and their regard for what is right before their principles and their regard for what is right before any personal advantage.

[1] Younger brother of King Louis XVI, executed 1792. Louis XVIII, b. 1755, reigned from 1814 until his death in 1824, apart from 'the Hundred Days', March-June 1815, when Napoleon Bonaparte returned to France but was defeated at Waterloo.

How often Ernest has been blamed, for having had the courage to defend against the mighty usurper the cause of the unfortunate King, who had so nobly refused to enlarge his Kingdom at our expense. Posterity will some day do him justice, when the oppressor and oppressed will have vanished from this world.

August 19th. May Sophie spend as happy a year as her birthday, which we have celebrated as festively as we could in the absence of her good husband. We had a "déjeuner" in Leopold's garden and a "diner" in dear Uncle's "Gartensalon." I am sure that if he knew, he would be pleased that his family should make use of what was one his. We had tea at Julie's, who had arranged a very pretty children's party and had filled her rooms with flowers. Alphonse and Hugo drove a little cart decorated with flowers in which sat their small brothers. They brought greetings and good wises from their father, who is so far away. When it got dark the garden was lit up with little lanterns and the drive to the entrance gate was prettily illuminated.

August 23rd. I had a nice letter to-day from Ernest, from Colmar, which gave me much pleasure. He is greatly charmed with the beauties of the countryside and its many nice towns and villages. The inhabitants have received the Saxons very well, and there has not been one discordant note.

September 16th. My sister, whose visit I have been expecting with great pleasure, arrived at 5 o'clock this morning. It does one's heart good to see her looking so well and cheerful. As there is so little room in my small house, she is living in the new bigger one, and the rooms which have been uninhabited so far, look so pretty and nicely furnished!

September 22nd. This afternoon, my brother and Harry passed through here, and came in for a moment, on their way to Julie at the Rosenau.

September 24th (in the morning). Yesterday was a lovely day and also a happy one. Soon after 7, I drove off to the Rosenau, where the entire family were assembled round the breakfast table. I wonder when dear Julie will spend her birthday here again? That uncertainty rather spoils one's pleasure. God bless her and grant her health and happiness. I returned home at 11. My house had been decorated with greenery and flowers, and Julie, her ladies, my brother, his son, and others from Coburg lunched with me. It was a real summer's day. At 5 we drove into town, where a small stage had been erected in the "Riesensaal." A few members of the Casino gave a very good performance of the "Quakers." This was followed by a prettily thought out Tableau with an appropriate Prologue. It referred to Julie's approaching departure and expressed the hope of seeing her here again. Just as we were getting ready to leave, Ferdinand suddenly made his appearance. It gave us tremendous pleasure. We first of all drove to the Rosenau, where they had illuminated the garden with little lanterns, which unfortunately, the wind kept blowing out. Only the moon continued to shine steadily, asserting its right to light up the sky. Supper was rather late, and we only got back home by midnight.

September 25th. On a lovely morning Louise and I drove into town, and with my brother and Harry went to see Sophie in the Thiergarten. She gave us breakfast. We also lunched with her, after which we drove to the Rosenau. It was so warm, that we were able to have tea out of doors.

October 6th. To-morrow Ferdinand leaves us. He has a brilliant future in front of him, but it means that our ways of life will now lie in different directions and I cannot help feeling a little sad at this thought. In future he will have his own home and family and live in a foreign land. Of course he will pay us visits, but it won't be quite the same thing as having him living under the same roof. I think that he sometimes feels this himself. God's blessing go with him in his new life, and may he find that all his hopes of happiness with his beloved fiancée may be realised. Perfect happiness is rare in these days.

October 10th. If it were not for my sister being with me, I should certainly not be spending these cold autumn days at Ketschendorf, but in her company they pass only too quickly and it is more cheerful and cosy than in the big empty Schloss. The long evenings in the pleasant bright little rooms, enlivened by intimate conversations, seem positively to fly by!

October 11th. To-day starts the big Russian advance, there will be much movement of troops and we shall have to expect many coming through here.

October 31st. Julie left this morning for Switzerland, whither she has gone with her whole Household, and I wonder when I shall see her again! Sophie accompanied her as far as Lichtenfels.

November 1st. Louise and I were sitting talking, ratter sadly about her departure next day, when we heard a noise on the road, and I ran to the window. It was Ernest and Mensdorff, who looked in for a moment. I am so glad they are here again. Ernest is looking remarkably well.

November 3rd (Coburg). My sister left me this morning in terrible weather. How I shall miss her! I drove into town at 10, leaving Ketschendorf for good this year. Mensdorff has brought a nephew with him, the son of his sister, Countess Brie, a very nice-looking boy of 16, thoroughly French in appearance. The Emperor of Austria has given Ernest the splendid "Meerfeld" Lancer Regiment: which is a great mark of favour! Camille Brie is to serve in this Regiment; his father had also been in the Austrian Army, years ago.

November 19th. The fine morning tempted me out for a walk, and I met our Grenadiers and Volunteer Jägers who have returned from a most bloodless campaign. They only had the trouble of going that long way and coming back again and in between whiles, were comfortably quartered in Alsace. The Officers, and also a Saxon Staff Officer, lunched at the Schloss.

December 9th. This is the ninth anniversary of my beloved husband's death, and his memory remains as fresh as ever in our hearts. It is the last time that I shall spend this day in the house in which he died, and in which I have remained for the last long nine years. With the coming year I shall start on a new chapter of my life, and for the second time I am leaving the Schloss. The 15 years I spent there were the most troubled and momentous ones of my life. Perhaps a calm evening may follow upon the stormy days, but I hardly dare hope for it. I pray God not to lay heavier burdens on my declining years, than I am fit to bear.

December 14th. A letter from Leopold has caused us all great joy. On the 7th he was with Julie, and will be here on his birthday.

December 16th. To the pleasure of dear Leopold spending his birthday with us in the old home, after two troubled years, is mingled the thought, that it may be for the last time. His fate may take him to the North or West, whatever it is will mean separation from us. I do not dare to express any wishes regarding his future — that lies in God's hands. I only pray he may be as happy as possible. We breakfasted in Ernest's rooms, and later, the brothers sang for quite a long time. Their voices sound so well together. This evening there is a masked ball.

December 24th. Christmas Eve was celebrated in Ernest's anteroom, and old and young received many nice gifts. Ernest and Sophie had arranged everything with their own hands. There was a beautiful Christmas tree which glittered cheerfully, and we spent a very happy evening with Ernest.

December 27th. Ernest went to Vienna this afternoon, to be present at Ferdinand's wedding.

December 31st. I close this year with deep thankfulness, for the quiet way in which it is ending, and with the hope that many another quiet one will follow. The storm once more started by Napoleon passed over very quickly, and it is to be hoped that this arch troublemaker has now disappeared for ever. That which was so fiercely fought for in past years, has been accomplished in this. It is true that many things have not turned out as well as we expected, but when was man's work ever perfect? God's hand has shown itself mightily in the shaping of the people's destiny and inclined the will of the nations towards peace. Once more at the end of the year, I thank Him for His goodness in preserving all my dear ones. Only kind old Uncle is no longer with us! May I in the coming year have further reason for thanking Him, and may He help me to bear whatever lies in front of me.

Coburg from the West

The Rosenau, Coburg

Victoire, Princess of Leiningen, later Duchess of Kent

Prince Leopold, later King of the Belgians, c.1816

Princess Beatrice in her last years

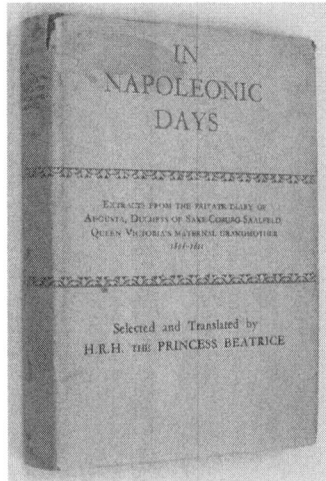

IN
NAPOLEONIC
DAYS

EXTRACTS FROM THE PRIVATE DIARY OF
AUGUSTA, DUCHESS OF SAXE-COBURG-SAALFELD
QUEEN VICTORIA'S MATERNAL GRANDMOTHER
1806-1821

Selected and Translated by
H.R.H. THE PRINCESS BEATRICE

The dust jacket of the original edition, published
by John Murray in 1941 in a green cloth binding

1816

January 2nd. I close this day, Ernest's birthday and Ferdinand's wedding day, with a thankful heart, and pray that God's blessing may rest on both. My mind has been filled all day with thoughts of the happy young couple, who are to-day starting their joint life together. Deep true love seals the bond, and may it endure many long years. How I hope that Ernest will one day find as good and charming a wife as his brother.

January 17th. It is only to-day that I have received a very old letter from Ernest from Vienna, fully participating in his brother's great happiness. The letter also contains details of the wedding. It took place in the Chapel of the Archbishop's Palace. The lovely young Bride, who was covered with jewels, looked like a rosebud. Duke Albert of Saxe-Teschen and Ernest accompanied Ferdinand to the altar.

January 19th. With a certain sense of melancholy, I begin this new year of my life, which is the first step into old age. God grant that the sun may shine upon it, dispelling all gloom and sense of loneliness and may my last years not be spent far from those dear to me. Good Sophie and her husband, the only ones of my children as to be near me, tried their utmost to make the day a happy one.

January 21st. When I returned this morning from my walk, Hohenbaum told me that an English courier had come to him and had made enquiries for Leopold. This probably means that his fate is being decided! In Thy hands it lies, oh God! I implicitly entrust his happiness to Thee. Even so my heart is sorrowful at the thought of a coming separation, which the advent of the courier brings nearer.

January 28th. To-day I read in the papers that a decision has been reached as to whom Princess Charlotte of Wales is to marry. With the approval of her father the Regent, and that of Parliament, the choice has fallen upon Prince Leopold of Saxe-Coburg. This news, which ought to make me proud, worries me very much. While I appreciate to the full the worth and noble characteristics of the young Princess, displayed in the strength and in the steadfast courageous manner in which for a year and a half she withstood her father's[1] persecution, remaining true to the first impression Leopold made upon her, I realise only too well what this marriage entails – Leopold's complete severance from his former existence and from us all and I do see and feel what the coming parting is going to mean to me, and cannot quite resign myself to it.

January 29th. Leopold has written that he will be here in a few days. The courier who came here had brought him an invitation from the Regent. Leopold will discuss all further details from me when we meet. He will only be able to spend a few days here, before the long separation that is before us.

February 2nd. Leopold arrived to-day and the pleasure of seeing him alone outweighed all other thoughts. But now that I am alone and quiet again, the dread of the impending separation returns to haunt me. Thy wisdom, oh God, has chosen this fate for Leopold, and has ordained that he should in time share the perils that beset a crowned head. Do Thou grant him strength and wisdom to tread this stormy path, and to me, grant courage to bear the parting and give me hope and faith in a reunion.

February 7th. The last day has come to an end! To-morrow Leopold quits for ever the dear old familiar home, with the memories of his carefree childhood and youth. His life will in future lie in more serious and responsible duties and soon the sea will form a barrier between his old life and his new life. Everything will be different, country, language, customs, etc. It is a very serious step to be taking. Oh Thou Ruler of the Universe, grant him a happy family life, which in high places is very rare, and may Charlotte, when she once ascends the throne, remain the same loving wife and trusted friend – only thus can his happiness be ensured. He always had a strong family

[1] George, Prince of Wales, Prince Regent and later King George IV.

feeling, and loved his simple home, to which he ever happily returned and surely now he will never forget us!

February 14th. Ernest arrived this afternoon quite unexpectedly from Berlin where he had seen Leopold, but only for a few days.

February 16th. Yesterday it was already a week since Leopold left us. It is lucky that time passes quickly even when the days are dreary. Leopold spent a few days with Victoire in Frankfort.

February 29th. To my great joy I received a letter from Leopold, from Calais, dated the 18th. Up to then, his journey over dreadful roads and in shocking weather had been very slow and dreary. Only at Cologne could he cross the Rhine, and from there he went via Aix-la-Chapelle, Brussels and the Netherlands to Calais, arriving there with a bad cold and cough in a storm which gave little hope of a good crossing.

March 2nd. A letter from Hardenbrock from Dover, reports that Leopold and he crossed over on the 19th of February leaving Calais at 4 in the afternoon and landing at 11. On account of the ebb tide, the boat could not enter the harbour and they had to go ashore in a "chaloupe," which grounded somewhat ungently on the chalk coast of Albion. Thank God! that they have got safely across, for in the terribly stormy weather, I was really anxious about the crossing.

March 8th. Both the weather and our life are very monotonous. Every day it rains and blows, and it is impossible to get out of the house. When the stormy evening succeeds the dreary day, we all foregather in my big room, and occupy ourselves in various ways.

March 12th. Again news from Leopold and very good news. He was received very cordially by the Regent in Brighton, and also by the old Queen,[1] who had brought Princess Charlotte with her, from Windsor. He seems in a very happy frame of mind. In accordance with English etiquette, he cannot go to London until the wedding.

[1] Charlotte, wife of King George III, daughter of Duke Charles of Mecklenburg Strelitz.

Meanwhile, he will go to Weymouth, where the rest, and perhaps some sea baths, may be beneficial for his health which has suffered a good deal from his many recent preoccupations.

March 27th. I cannot describe the feeling with which I read in the papers the praise of Leopold. It was in a speech of Lord Castlereagh's[1] in Parliament when he announced to that body, in the Regent's name, the betrothal of Princess Charlotte. With true maternal pride and joy I thanked God, that all the British Minister said in praise of Leopold was true. He may be envied for his good luck but even his detractors, if such there are, must recognise his merit and singleness of heart.

April 7th. Victoire and her children arrived this afternoon and I am delighted to have them once again with me under the old paternal roof. Charles and Feodore have not grown very much, but look the picture of health.

April 26th. Leopold writes that his wedding was ultimately fixed for the 26th, so it is to-day that the peace and happiness of his life is to be decided. All day my thoughts have been taken up with this great event. Now in the quiet evening hour I picture to myself the tall figure of my dear son with his gentle face, probably rather pale, standing beside the handsome, high-spirited daughter of Kings and receiving the blessing which binds him to the future Sovereign of Great Britain. It is a great task which he undertakes.

May 13th. A letter from the old Queen of England contains the information that the wedding did not after all take place till the 2nd. She wrote to me the very day after, and I am much touched by this kind attention on her part.

May 19th. To-day a salute of guns was fired and a Thanksgiving Service was held to celebrate Leopold's happiness, and how heartily I joined in the Thanksgiving Hymn.

[1] Robert Stewart, Viscount Castlereagh, Leader of the House of Commons.

May 20th (Ketschendorf). At last I have settled here. It is later than I have ever done so before. We had tea in the garden, and when all had left, I roamed about my garden, delighting in the peace and quietness of this little country home, which I never seem to have appreciated so much before.

May 28th. Ernest rode off early with Solms to Gotha and from morning till night it did nothing but rain.

May 29th. In the early hours of the morning Mensdorff also went to Gotha, but luckily he had fine weather.

May 31st. Ernest and Mensdorff returned to-day from Gotha in heavy rain. They were very pleased with their journey. I should not be surprised if I did not soon have a daughter from there. God's blessing be with the project, provided it is for his happiness. In a couple of days he is going to Salzburg to the Emperor of Austria.

June 6th. To-morrow I am going to Lobenstein and Victoire, in another few days, to Ebersdorf.

June 10th. It is too despairing, the rain never ceases! However, in the peasant atmosphere of my sister and her children's family party, and the pretty cheerful rooms, one quite forgets that it is trying to be November in June! It is sad to see this attractive part of the world spoilt by such horrid weather.

June 17th. The Ebersdorf family with Victoire and her children came over to luncheon, in wretched weather. Mensdorff has received orders to proceed to Prague where he will be informed of further decisions. I am very sorry for this and it will quite sadden my return home to-morrow.

June 19th (Coburg). Mensdorff's approaching departure makes me very sad, although I had foreseen for some time that this was likely to happen. Sophie and the dear boys will also be leaving soon. At 6 to-day Victoire and Ernest arrived together, having met at Lichtenfels. Ernest is delighted with the incomparable beauty of the position of Salzburg and the whole romantic scenery there. The

Emperor received him most cordially and made him many promises. In Munich, too, he had met with a very kind welcome.

June 29th. At last there is news of Ferdinand, who with his young wife expects to be here on July 2nd. What a pleasure this will be for me!

June 30th. This morning I began my preparations for the move from the Schloss to my charming new abode, which Ernest has arranged so prettily for me. While I was busily occupied in unpacking and arranging my things, there came a letter from Ferdinand, saying he and his wife would now arrive to-day, and this news flustered me a good deal. After luncheon, Caroline, little Feodore and I drove to Ketschendorf, Sophie and Victoire going to meet the travellers. We waited for them on the balcony. Soon the post master rode up with the postillions blowing their horns and a few local guards. These were followed shortly by Ernest and his Gentlemen. The young couple arrived at 7, and much moved, I warmly embraced my dear pretty daughter-in-law. A very true saying of Golowkin's came to my mind: "on est tenté de chercher les ailes en la regardant!" Tony[1] (as she is called) possesses quite an ethereal kind of beauty and is indescribably attractive. Ferdinand seemed radiant at being able to present his charming wife to us.

July 1st. I cannot sufficiently feast my eyes on the dear daughter Ferdinand has brought into our family. Her chief charm consists in the beautiful sweet kindly expression of her eyes. She seems so simple and unspoilt, quite incapable of any wrong or unkind action and so youthful and innocent. This childlike attitude combined with great good sense and intelligence makes her a very interesting character. We lunched quite "en famille" at the Schloss, and in lovely weather had tea and supper here.

July 2nd. Tony celebrates to-day her 19th birthday. May God's blessing follow her through life.

---

[1] Antoinette Gabriele, wife of Prince Ferdinand, daughter of Prince Francis of Cohary.

July 3rd. Yesterday's birthday was celebrated by a Banquet in the Riesensaal and in the evening there was a pretty little fête in the old Gallery, which Renier the French architect had decorated very tastefully with greenery and garlands composed only of cornflowers.

July 10th. At midnight I returned from a charming fête at the Rosenau. Peasants came with a band to dance in front of the house, after having first welcomed Tony in the valley. This had to take place later than was planned, owing to a thunderstorm, and dawn was already approaching. We had supper in the cosy little saloon, and later we went out and saw some very successful illuminations. The whole thing was quite fairy like and the moon gleamed fitfully through clouds.

July 18th. Victoire is leaving us in two days. The three months that she has spent with us have passed by like a day, and she will leave a great blank in our family circle. These ever-recurring separations are to me one of the nightmares of life.

July 20th. On a beautiful summer's morning we accompanied Victoire as far as Simau, lunching with her there in a garden. She left directly afterwards. I am hoping to see her again in the autumn, but even so, the parting cost me a good deal.

July 25th. I went on foot from Ketschendorf into the town, to visit Sophie, who has had to leave her rooms in the Schloss as building is going on in that wing. She now occupies Julie's house. We lunched in Ferdinand's "Gartenhaus," and he seemed to enjoy entertaining us in his own domain.

July 31st. For the first time I had my children to a meal in my new house. It was a cheerful little party. Tony and the other ladies remained on, the gentlemen rejoining us for tea.

August 6th. Ernest left early this morning for Eger, on business, and will await Ferdinand there.

August 7th. I have just returned with a heavy heart from Ketschendorf where Tony and Ferdinand have been spending their last evening. As twilight approached we all felt sadder and sadder, and the strains of a band which Ferdinand had ordered made it even worse. I love his dear young wife with my whole heart. She, on her side, seems to leave her husband's family and old home, to which he was so attached, with real regret.

August 19th. Sophie began her birthday very happily, for the first thing she saw besides her children, was her good excellent husband. Before I had time to go round to her room, they both came to me, and my pleasure was almost as great as hers, to see this dear son, of whom I am so fond. Caroline gave a little "déjeuner" and Mensdorff, Sophie, their children and their tutor lunched with me. I had my rooms festively decorated with greenery and pots of hydrangeas, which had a very pretty effect. In the afternoon we went to Ketschendorf, where the children acted a little play.

November 1st. A month ago to-day I left that charming place Elfenau and have just driven into the old town of Basle. I shall never forget my pleasant stay at Elfenau.

November 18th. This afternoon, the Count Chamberlain, Count Salish, arrived from Gotha to see Ernest and explain to him with many excuses that for the present the discussions about the betrothal could not proceed any further. The state of the Duchess's health has prevented her leaving Jena sooner and for the same reason there could be no celebrations of the Duke's birthday. I am somewhat upset and perturbed, and whenever I think of that marriage, I have a sort of secret dead, that nothing may come of it.

December 16th. May God's richest blessings rest on dear Leopold, on this the first birthday he spends in England, and for the remainder of his life! Much as the separation weighs on my mind, I dare not complain, for Leopold is happy. He has not suffered, as I feared he might, from the irksome constraint of court etiquette, or from cabals, difficult to avoid in a marriage to one so near the throne. No, he is genuinely happy and satisfied with his family life, which is like that of any other private person is spent with a wife to whom he is devoted, in the surroundings of a charming country home. Only in England is it possible for the husband of the heiress to the throne to lead the happy unfettered life of a private gentleman. May God preserve to him this rare happiness of wedded life founded on mutual trust and affection.

December 17th. Ernest is now going to Gotha in two days' time, I hope to be betrothed.

December 21st. We were sitting this afternoon with Sophie, discussing Ernest's prospects when a messenger arrived with the news that his betrothal had taken place already yesterday. His news gives me much pleasure, though it came in no wiser as a surprise. How I hope that the union may prove a happy one for both parties. May Ernest find in his pretty young bride, Louise,[1] a true and devoted life companion, and possibly in the future a wise competent mother of his children, also now in the heyday of his youth, a loving wife.

December 25th. Ernest's engagement was celebrated to-day with joy and true thankfulness. May God bless this union and may each be patient with the other and treat with leniency any little differences or weaknesses that may arise; may mutual trust abide with them unto their life's end.

December 31st. To-day ends this first year spent in my pleasant new dwelling and I look back with deep thankfulness to all God's blessings and mercies. It has been a very important year for me: Ferdinand and Leopold have both got married, and Ernest is engaged to be married, I can only pray that the latter may be as happy as his brothers and that all may retain their happiness. What pleasant moments I have passed in this year, though also sad ones, as in the case of my separation from Leopold. Who could have dared hope that he would have found with Charlotte simple married happiness, as is now his, and that she should have proved herself so worthy of him. But I really cannot enumerate the number of blessings I have to thank God for.

[1] Louise (b. December 21, 1800), daughter and heiress of Duke Augustus of Saxe-Coburg-Gotha. Owing to this marriage the family of Saxe-Coburg-Saalfeld became that of Saxe-Coburg-Gotha.

1817

January 19th. I begin this day with deep thankfulness towards God, Who has so mercifully brought me through many a sorrow and trial to the threshold of old age. I am already 60. How fast time has gone by, but I should not care to live over again those long years, which appear to me now as a dream. With the same feelings of thankfulness I go trustfully forward into the unknown. I have only still one wish, which I pray may be granted me, and that is that I may not outlive my reasoning faculties!

March 10th. I have to-day received a very fine portrait of Charlotte depicting in her face her youthful beauty and high spirit, also showing an expression of kindness, openness and determination which cannot fail to fascinate one.

March 13th (Ketschendorf). I have not been able to withstand any longer the call of the nightingales and spring, and remained here for the night, for the first time. When I move into town in the autumn, the time spent until I return again here to my peaceful little home seems like an eternity. But the seasons and months pass so quickly I hardly realise how fast the time flies.

July 17th. This afternoon I got a letter from Ferdinand, announcing his arrival this evening. There is no possibility of putting him and Tony up in the Schloss, so I have arranged as best I can, to lodge them up in my house, which is however not very commodious. They arrived at 6, Ferdinand looking well, and my dear daughter-in-law Tony, as pretty and blooming as a year ago.

July 21st. In heavenly weather, we went to the Rosenau, where Ferdinand and Tony were very pleased with some improvements to the dear charming place.

July 27th. This afternoon, Ernest, Ferdinand and Mensdorff, went on horseback through the woods to Gotha, spending the night in Ohrdruf, in order to make their solemn entry into Gotha to-morrow morning. The Chief Chamberlain had already gone there yesterday, as well as the other Gentlemen. How I hope all will go well, and that the important step Ernest is taking may be for his lasting happiness.

July 31st. My first and last thoughts to-day have been of Ernest, whose marriage was to take place this evening at 6. Do Thou, oh God, bless this union and grant that they may find all happiness in their home life!

August 2nd. I lunched alone with Tony at Ketschendorf and we were joined in the afternoon by Caroline and Sophie, who came to await Victoire's arrival. She had spent the night at Bamberg, and only got here at 5 accompanied by Feodora and Fräulein Späth. We drove together into town, Tony hoping to see her husband, who only arrived at half-past ten.

August 3rd. I had half the town to tea, as all were wishing to offer their congratulations, on Ernest's marriage.

August 7th. May God's blessing rest on the dear young couple, who have entered Ernest's ancestral home to-day. May peace, contentment and good health attend them throughout life and may the in their old age be able to look back on this day, with joy and satisfaction.

August 8th. I was unable to write more yesterday, as I was too agitated and tired. The day was beautiful from the earliest hours and the new home was decked out in summer splendour, to receive the young bride. There were signs of life and animation in the whole town and in surroundings, and people busy carrying branches of foliage or flowers to make wreaths for the adornment of triumphal arches. Already at 4 the sounds of guns announced that the couple had just passed Fuchsberg; Sophie drove with her husband and eldest boy to near Neuses to meet and welcome her sister-in-law, so did Ferdinand and Tony, who looked too sweet, all dressed in pink. Caroline, Victoire and I went into the Schloss to receive the young couple, but had to wait till half-past six, when the procession which had slowly wended its way through the town, amidst the firing of guns and ringing of bells, at last appeared. Ernest and his wife drove in an open carriage. They were preceded and followed by detachments of troops, all the foresters, members of different guilds, etc. The Master of the Horse and other Court Officials rode beside the carriage. The Guard of Honour was drawn up on the "Pelouse" and people of all classes stood in the open "Platz." The poor little wife was so agitated and "émotionnée" that she could hardly speak. She is a dear, sweet little person, not exactly pretty, but very attractive in her extreme youth and vivacity. She has expressive large blue eyes and a pleasant voice. She speaks well with much good sense and is most amiable, so that one must like her. I hope she will grow a little for she is very short. This afternoon there was a big reception "Cour" and banquet. Louise in her wedding dress, heavily embroidered in silver, and wearing many jewels looked more imposing than pretty and the silver made her appear rather pale. We had tea here, and as the evening was so fine and warm, we remained sitting on the balcony until 9 o'clock.

August 9th. Ernest brought his dear little wife quite early to see me., she looked very sweet in her simple morning dress. They lunched with me, and in the evening there was a most brilliant ball in the "Riesensaal."

August 12th. To-day one of the most successful fêtes I ever remember took place at the Rosenau; it was a Carousel, which was held on a big "Platz," facing the house and the lovely view opposite the hills. Round the barriers, sat and stood a vast concourse of people. The sight from our tribune was really charming. All the persons belonging to the Court were attired in ancient German costumes, including the ladies and the gentlemen of my family, who all looked extremely well. The procession came from the Rosenau across the meadows. First came trumpeters, then esquires, after them two heralds in tabbards holding staves and two pages followed by riders in pairs. Ernest was superb in silver and golden armour and other fine accoutrements. Ferdinand also looked very well. The second couple were Mensdorff and Coburg, etc. There were all kinds of pageantry, jousts with lances and swords, etc., and then trumpeters and esquires rode in again and Knights performed various figures in a Musical Ride. Everything went off with great precision and order, there was not a single hitch and no unruly horse spoilt the general effect.

August 19th. Sophie started her birthday in a strange way! At 5 o'clock in the morning she became the mother of a fine little boy. My joy and thankfulness are beyond words. Mother and child are well. God bless them both!

August 23rd. I was just going to see Sophie, when I received the news of Julie's arrival and I hurried joyfully to greet her. She is delighted to be with us again. In the afternoon, Ernest and Ferdinand with their wives came over here, and we all had tea together.

August 24th. Sophie is not at all well and I am very anxious particularly in view of her rather delicate nerves.

August 29th. What a fearful afternoon I have just been through, driven wild by my anxiety for Sophie! When I got to her bedside I found her in a state of nervous collapse, from which she occasionally revived, but never quite regained consciousness. The Doctors considered her condition most serious, and only one step short of some sort of paralysis! Towards evening her head became clearer and she spoke a few words sensibly. God be praised, she is no longer in any immediate danger, though there are still worrying symptoms.

September 5th. The night was good and Sophie's head is quite clear, this morning. It is the ninth day of her illness. After luncheon I drove with Victoire to the Rosenau to say goodbye, as she is leaving to-morrow.

September 10th. Thank God! the improvement in Sophie's condition becomes daily more marked. After luncheon I fetched Julie and we drove up to the "Festung" where Ernest and the whole of the Rosenau party came to take tea. The beautiful view lay bathed in sunshine. As we drove round the old place we heard sounds of horns above us, which made one think of olden days, when they must often have sounded to welcome Knights to a Tournament. It was a glorious evening and the lower the sun sank the more beautiful did the distant view get.

September 16th. With a sad heart I part to-morrow from Ferdinand and Tony. When shall I see these dear children again? Ferdinand was so well and happy, quite his old self, and Tony more lovable and merry as ever. I think it also costs her a good deal to tear herself away from us, for she seems to love me, much as if she were my old child. Ernest and Louise, Ferdinand and his wife and Julie with her ladies lunched with me on the balcony. We took tea with Julie.

September 17th. I had only a few moments this morning with the dear travellers before, to my infinite regret, I saw them drive away in miserable wet weather.

September 18th. Sophie passed a fairly good day. Her strength is returning slowly, and she is improving daily. To-day she was able to move the poor stricken left arm and foot, but I fear it will still take a long time, before she can regain the proper use of her limbs. If only the autumn was not already so far advanced she might have gone to some watering place, where baths would have been sure to put her right again in a far shorter time.

September 23rd. Oh, why must the pleasure of having Julie here for her birthday, be spoilt by the thought of her imminent departure? In the afternoon we drove to the Rosenau, but unfortunately the weather was dull and rainy. The dining-room was very festively decorated with flowers and plants. After dinner we sat out for a short time to see the illuminations in the garden, but were soon driven in by the damp. The evening ended in a cheerful dance.

September 25th. I end this day, saddened by having had to part once more from Julie. It is such a pity that she should have made the long journey for such a short time, and most of her visit was spoilt, by the incessant anxiety about poor Sophie.

October 14th. Thank goodness Sophie is getting daily better. She can now walk quite alone and has been twice out driving, which evidently has done her much good.

October 17th. I had hardly finished my little solitary luncheon when Sophie drove up and spent half an hour with me sitting on the balcony in the pleasant afternoon sun. It was nice to see her sitting out again, after her serious illness.

October 31st. The 300th jubilee of the Reformation was kept here with great solemnity, as it was all over Germany. Ernest and Louise together with several of the latter's ladies came from Rodach into town for a few days. There was a big dinner at the Schloss. At the Commemoration Service to-day the new young Court Chaplain preached a very suitable and wise sermon.

November 9th. After twelve long weeks Sophie was churched to-day, but she was not yet able to kneel. I called to mind all the terrible hours of suspense we went through and the pathetic and heartrending Christening of little Arthur. How I thanked God for having so mercifully preserved my dear daughter from such danger. She looked wonderfully well, considering what she has been through, but afterwards she was a little tired. I went to tea at the Schloss. Ernest and Louise live in the small rooms in the new wing, which look very cheerful and pretty, lit up in the evening.

November 13th. I am daily waiting with anxiety and impatience the arrival of the Courier, bringing the news of Charlotte's confinement.

November 16th. The Courier has come — Charlotte is dead![1] I am quite overcome by the enormity of this calamity! Poor dear Leopold! I feel quite ill and can hardly think or write! All day I have been thinking in despair of the kind fine woman, of whom we were so proud, and whose going has shattered all the hopes of happiness of poor Leopold's life. The ways of Providence are indeed inscrutable and it is difficult to understand why this beautiful young creature should be cut off, on the very threshold of life, taking her child with her.

November 22nd. I have written again to Leopold and wanted to do so every day, but when I took up the pen, I did not seem able to find adequate words for such a terrible misfortune as has befallen him. It was like lightning out of a blue sky, for who could ever have thought

[1] Princess Charlotte of Wales died on 6 November after giving birth to a stillborn son.

141

that this healthy young woman would only survive her confinement a few hours. It entered no one's head to anticipate such a disaster. And now my poor son stands alone in foreign country amid the ruins of his shattered happiness. All the joys of a sweet companionship and calm married life, in a delightful home, as well as the interest of planning for Charlotte's future, are now at an end. Charlotte's noble and impetuous nature had learnt to rely on Leopold's wise and cautious counsel and his unusually cool judgment. What a sad outlook for the poor man who has lost so much and what can the future still hold for him?

November 25th. I am anxiously awaiting letters from England, and yet I dread them. All the papers speak of Leopold's speechless misery and of the deep grief of the whole nation at the loss of the Heiress to the Crown. Oh, why had mother and child to die together? Oh God, Who hast laid this trial upon me, give me strength not to question Thy wisdom!

November 27th. Dreary rainy November days succeed each other and my days pass by monotonously. I cannot go to the Schloss, on account of a swollen foot, but my children come to see me daily.

December 9th. To-day on the anniversary of his death the remains of the late lamented Duke have been removed to the newly built place of burial. He had wished so much that this should be done, so his son, in filial obedience, has carried out his desire. Yesterday I received a letter from Leopold, so miserable and utterly crushed, that I could not read his words without tears.

December 19th. What a storm, and what snow! I cannot leave the house and a very quiet evening, only relieved by the presence of Caroline, falls in with my present mood. When one gets old one is so thankful to be quiet.

December 21st. Louise has kept her seventeenth birthday very happily to-day and may she likewise spend her eighteenth birthday! Her extreme youth and air of fragility, make the thought of her becoming a mother rather anxious and the recent loss of Charlotte has made me nervous. I found the young couple at breakfast when I went to wish Louise joy. At 11 I gave a small "déjeuner" at my house and there was a big dinner at Court. In the evening there was a very successful theatrical performance.

December 24th. I come from Sophie who had a Christmas tree for her children and it is wonderful that she was able to arrange this, and organise everything to amuse them.

December 31st. I have spent this last day of the year with many a sad thought principally occupied with Leopold and the terrible sorrow which has annihilated his happiness at the end of one year. Even Antoinette's arrival, which naturally is a great pleasure to me, has not been able entirely to dispel the gloom. In this year we have experienced great mercies at God's hands, but also grievous trouble. He has given me a new daughter this year, and I pray she may be preserved, through the painful ordeal which she will have to undergo in a few months' time. I thank God, that after such a dangerous illness Sophie has been given back to her husband and children. Of course she is not yet what she was, but I pray that in the new year she may quite regain her strength. I myself feel this winter the weight of years pressing heavily upon me, and my one dread is lest the rheumatic gout I suffer from, may perhaps soon deprive me of my one pleasure, that of wandering about, in God's beautiful world. But I know I have no right to complain.

1 8 1 8

January 2nd. To-day Ernest has for the first time for four years spent his birthday again here, and his dear amiable little wife has done all in her power to celebrate it worthily. Louise gave a "déjeuner" in the morning, and they lunched with me. In the evening there were Tableaux of episodes in the Saxon History and they were very well done, the grouping, the costumes and the lighting, all equally good. A pretty little stage had been erected in the "Riesensaal" and everything charmingly planned throughout.

January 7th. Poor Leopold, with what feelings will he have spent to-day, which was Charlotte's birthday! I have been thinking of him all day and of his unutterable grief.

January 8th. There was a great shoot at the Rosenau to-day. Ernest and Louise lunched there, and Victoire with Fräulein Späth came to me. In the evening we took tea in the Schloss. One day resembles another. In the mornings Victoire remains with me and we spend the afternoons at the Schloss. We often dine there.

January 19th. For the second time, I spend my birthday in this quiet house, which I find so attractive and comfortable. I was awakened by music, and the first thing I saw, on entering my sitting-room, was a drawing of Leopold and Charlotte together. Victoire had had it copied from a drawing in her possession. I could hardly look at it without tears in my eyes. Victoire came to see me with Ernest and Louise at 11. After a little while I was summoned to my green dining-room, where I found a fine piece of furniture in dark wood, Ernest's gift, and a table from Louise. Mensdorff, Sophie and the dear boys as well as Caroline, all brought presents. Later I gave a déjeuner to which I invited, as well as my family, Frau von Wangenheim, Coburg and the Duchess's Ladies.

January 21st. Letters from the Duke of Kent to Victoire and Ernest make quite clear his intention of asking for her hand. In October 1816 and last year she could not make up her mind, but now she is much inclined to accept and looks forward calmly to a new life. I will not interfere in this affair, but leave my daughter's future abut which I am rather anxious, in God's hands. Since Charlotte was taken from us, I seem to feel that happiness is insecure and dare not hope too much for joyous days.

January 26th. How quickly the nice days have flown, which Victoire has spent with us. It made me so happy to have her all to myself, quietly living with me. She left me this morning. Dear, good child, she seems so unperturbed at what lies before her and this almost worries me. In a few months' time, she may possibly become the wife of a man she hardly knows. If it is God's will that this union should take place may He watch over her, for the marriage is certainly not of her own seeking.

April 12th. Most unexpectedly Mr. Taylor, the English Minister at Stuttgart, arrived to-day, on the Duke of Kent's business. In England everything is going according to his wishes. The Regent and the Queen consent, and the whole of the country approve the marriage, Leopold being much liked.

May 25th. Victoire came to-day, and is living with me for the last time, as Princess of Leiningen.

May 26th. We had only expected the Duke of Kent to-morrow, but hardly had we sat down to luncheon, when a Courier arrived with the news that the Duke would follow in two hours. We waited with much curiosity and poor Victoire with a beating heart. She had only seen him once before. At 4 o'clock he arrived with the English Minister in Stuttgart, Taylor, two Gentlemen from the Legation; Knatchbull and Barnard and Colonel Hervey who is waiting on the Duke. At first the Duke, man of the world though he is, was somewhat embarrassed at suddenly breaking in on our large family circle. He is a fine man for his age, has a pleasant winning manner, and a good-humoured expression. His tall stature helps to give him an air of breeding, and he combines a simple soldierly manner with the refinement of a man of the world, which makes intercourse with him easy and pleasant. We all had tea here, and went to supper at the Schloss.

May 27th. We lunched at the Rosenau, with which the Duke of Kent was much pleased, and everyone came to supper with me.

May 28th. At 1, I drove with Victoire "en cérémonie" to the Schloss for her Betrothal. We ladies awaited the Duke of Kent in the State Rooms. He was accompanied by Ernest and preceded by gentlemen in attendance. The future married couple exchanged rings. Then followed a big "diner" and in the evening a rather tedious concert!

May 30th (in the morning). Yesterday was Victoire's wedding-day, but I was too agitated and exhausted to be able to do any writing late in the evening. Victoire, Louise, Sophie and Späth lunched with me, and in the evening, at half-past eight, we again drove "en cérémonie" to the Schloss, going into one of the State Rooms, where Ernest awaited his sister. The Duke of Kent was already standing under a velvet canopy, in the brilliantly lit Riesensaal. He looked very well in his English Field-Marshal's uniform and Victoire, charming, in a white dress trimmed with white roses and orange blossoms. With complete faith, I placed my beloved daughter's future in God's hands. May the dear good child find in this second marriage all the happiness which she had not quite attained in this last one and may His blessing follow her. A salute from the "Festung" proclaimed that the ceremony had been accomplished. We then returned to the State Rooms, after which, rather late, there was a State Dinner. I accompanied the newly married couple to their apartments, which had been charmingly prepared for them. When I got back home, I felt thoroughly tired out.

June 1st. Taylor and the two Gentlemen who accompanied the Duke of Kent left early this morning. He is a most agreeable man and his two companions were gentlemanly, unassuming young men.

June 2nd. On a very hot morning, Ernest, the Duke of Kent, Mensdorff and Colonel Hervey rode up to the "Festung" and were greeted by a salute of guns. We lunched in the "Hofgarten" and spent the evening in Mensdorff's garden. We had a family supper in Victoire's apartments. To-morrow the newly married couple leave. I

146

hope Victoire will be happy with he really very amiable husband, who only in middle age, makes acquaintance with family life and will therefore perhaps appreciate it all the more.

June 4th (Ketschendorf). For the first time I am spending the night here. I have never settled to late before.

June 5th. The Duchess of Gotha[1] came to-day. She is still so good-looking and most friendly and courteous.

June 8th. We lunched at the Hofgarten and I went for a walk, until it was time to dress for the Curt. It was rather long and wearisome, and was followed by an equally wearisome concert.

June 21st. God be praised! Louise has been happily delivered of a healthy son.[2] Only a few minutes before, I had received a letter from Ferdinand announcing that Tony had also safely given birth to a son.[3] How grateful I am to Providence, for this double joy. All this news has quite excited me. At 10, there was a Thanksgiving Service in the "Stadtkirche," to the accompaniment of ringing of bells and firing of guns. After luncheon, I fled back here, to try to get a little sleep, for the joy of the good people of Coburg expresses itself so noisily that I really could not stand it any longer! Later, I went again into town to see Louise, who with her little boy is as well as one could wish.

June 25th. On a lovely morning Sophie and Mensdorff left for Carlsbad. May she pick up her health again there!

July 4th. The Duke of Gotha arrived early this morning and has grown so stout that I hardly recognised him.

July 5th. Weary and tired, I close this unforgettable day, when our little boy was christened. The Ceremony was one of the most impressive I have ever seen. We drove in state to the "Stadtkirche"

[1] Caroline Amelia, daughter of the Kurfürst William I of Hesse, 2nd wife of the Duke Augusta of Saxe-Gotha.
[2] Afterwards the reigning Duke Ernest, d. 1893.
[3] Prince Augustus.

which was beautifully decorated with flowers and greenery. Ernest asked the country to stand sponsor to his first-born and the different towns, societies, and guilds etc., sent Deputations to attend the Christening. We stood in a circle in front of the Chancel, the Duke, the beautifully dressed Duchess of Gotha, Caroline, the Deputations and myself. It was a touching sight when one of the Court Ladies, attired in silver brocade, placed in the arms of the simple peasant his little godson, whilst all the others beamed upon him with affection. God grant that the pleasure at the birth of this dear child may be justified hereafter. Ernest was much moved. There was a long, wearisome dinner in the Riesensaal, which was open to the public. Tea and supper were here, so as to spare the little mother as much fatigue as possible.

July 7th. The morning being very fine, Ernest breakfasted with me here at Ketschendorf. In the afternoon, the elder boys lunched with me in the garden, and I took tea at the Schloss to pay my farewell visit. Louise seemed sad at the thought of my going away for some weeks.

July 10th. Carlsbad is packed and it was difficult to find accommodation. This morning I went with Mensdorff to the Neubrunnen. What extraordinary people of all nationalities and classes one saw running about with glasses in their hands! I found several acquaintances.

July 11th. I went again to the springs, and walked up and down for some time with friends and finally, ready to drop, sat down on a bench. I have found some acquaintances of Antoinette's and it is a great joy to me to hear her praises sung by all the Russians and Livonians I have met.

August 13th. This is my last day at Carlsbad, and I am feeling rather tired by my cure. I have been hearing Catalani sing, she has the most heavenly voice. I never heard such purity, such flexibility combined with such feeling and such a single way of singing. It has made quite an impression on me, and I shall never forget it.

August 16th (Coburg). I was thankful to find all my dear ones here, in good health, and to get a letter from Victoire, telling me she was happy in England.

September 10th. To-morrow, Ernest and Louise start on their journey to Dresden. They will spend a few days in Saalfeld, and on the 15th Louise will go to Runneburg, in order to travel with her mother to Dresden. Poor Ernest has to make a flying visit to Berlin, in order to see the Emperor of Russia, and will rejoin Louise in Dresden on the 19th. From there they intend going to Bohemia to visit the "Ernst Regiment" at Saatz. The young parents feel very much parting from their dear little son, who is left at the Rosenau. They also much regret coming away from there, in this lovely weather.

September 11th. The travellers are lucky in having glorious weather to-day. I am so glad, as the good people of Saalfeld have been making such great preparations for their reception.

September 13th. A letter from Ernest informs me that the Empress Elisabeth is coming here on the 28th. Ernest is now going with Louise to Dresden and has given up the journey to Berlin, as he is to meet the Russian Emperor at Weimar where he will await the Empress.

September 22nd. After having waited in vain the whole of yesterday for Leopold's arrival, a messenger came early this morning with a letter from him, saying that Prince William of Prussia had given him a "rendez-vous" and that he could only get here on the 28th. This news puts me out a good deal, as this means Leopold and the Empress will arrive together. Pleased as I am to see Elisabeth, it will be very disturbing to have her there at my first meeting with Leopold since his bereavement.

September 23rd. Another messenger came this morning and Leopold's arrival is again put off as he is going, on the way, to see Julie and wishes to spend her birthday with her.

September 29th. Ernest arrived in the afternoon from Saalfeld, and the Empress yesterday evening. To-day Louise brings her here. Ernest came to see me in the garden, where he was joined by Sophie, Mensdorff and their children. We hurried to dress, as the Empress was expected at 6 and I got to the Schloss soon after. The whole Court was assembled there and also some outsiders. We waited over an hour and a half. At last the thunder of guns and ringing of bells announced the arrival of the Empress. Night had come on and the outriders had to carry torches. There were many more torches in the Courtyard, which gave rather a fantastic appearance to the scene. I went into the Hall to receive the Empress. She is always the same — so friendly and gracious to us. I do not find her at all altered.

September 30th. It was a fine morning when the Empress came first to my house which she wished to see, and then drove with Ernest and Louise to Ketschendorf. I hurried on before them to get there in time to receive them. Elisabeth seemed much pleased with the house and its surroundings, which were looking their best in the brilliant sunlight. We were sitting on the balcony cosily chatting, when the Duke of Bavaria passed through Ketschendorf in order to invite the Empress to luncheon at Banz the following day. In the afternoon we drove to the Rosenau, from which we returned late. Before the "souper" there was to be a presentation of ladies but the kind Empress would not let this interfere with her taking tea with me, and when she left to return to the Schloss she would not hear of my accompanying her, for which I was very thankful, as I was feeling very tired. This reminds me how old I am getting.

October 1st. The Empress left this morning at 10, and already at half-past eight I was at the Schloss and we sat talking together for some time. She is so charming and simple, taking interest in the smallest things, never in the least condescending, though quite able to play the part of a great Empress, when necessary. But from her gentle somewhat melancholy expression one gathers that she is not very happy and that she bears her troubles with calm resignation. That her sister-in-law gave a son to the country was not the least of her trials. Ernest accompanied her to Banz.

October 5th. Leopold is here! I am infinitely glad to see him, but greatly shocked at the great change in my pet, and I could hardly hide my emotion. The dear face bears the imprint of a deep sorrow. How different it would all have been could he have brought Charlotte with him!

October 6th. It is delightful having Leopold living here. He breakfasted with me this morning as in the good old days. We lunched at the Schloss "en famille" and all came to tea and supper with me, including Leopold's Gentlemen.

October 16th. We are having marvellous weather and one hardly likes to be indoors the air is so delicious. The Gentlemen, who had been shooting at the Rosenau, returned so late, that we only sat down to luncheon after 4, quite famished. The beautiful sunset suggested to Ernest the idea of having tea at Ketschendorf, so Louise, Leopold and I drove there directly after luncheon. Twilight was falling, but the woods and hills were still bathed in a rosy glow. We came back rather late in beautiful moonlight

October 18th. The sharp north-east wind which began already yesterday has made such a change in the temperature that even in the brightest sunshine it was bitterly cold. Special prayers of Thanksgiving were offered up in Church for the great blessings that the 18th of October 1813 brought to the whole of Germany and please God may they continue! In celebration of the day the Guild of Marksmen had an exhibition of shooting and we lunched at the Range. It was a very pleasant party and the sun shone quite warmly into the tent. Shooting competitions were held afterwards. Everybody came again to tea in my house.

October 20th. The whole Court, as well as Leopold, went to-day to Rodach, the gentlemen intending to shoot.

October 24th (Rodach). After the lapse of many years, I have for the first time again spent a night here. Ernest and Louise have begged me to stay on a few days. The house is very nicely arranged, only some of the rooms on the ground floor reminding one of past days. I am lodged in what used to be my children's nursery.

October 25th. The weather to-day was heavenly, really more of a summer, than an autumn day. I went alone with the gentlemen to church, as Louise was not feeling very well. The little church reminded me so forcibly of bygone days! The old clergyman preached a fine sermon. Of course the congregation which filled the church must have belonged entirely to a new generation. I walked across the meadows, where many a time I had walked with my husband and small children in former days. Everything is quite unchanged and I recalled the past, with a certain feeling of melancholy. Oh, if only those happy old days could return again!

November 6th. Leopold has come into town to-day, to spend quietly the first anniversary of his great loss. He was bearing it with manly courage, but he looked very pale and drawn, and I could see how much he was suffering. I tacitly sympathised with him, but how could anyone comfort him? Time alone can by degrees heal the wound of which he will bear the scar to the grave. He is still so young that one must hope that there is some brightness in store for him.

November 19th. Since the 15th I have been expecting Julie daily. To-day she at last arrived, with her whole Household, to spend the winter with us. I have been so looking forward to this great pleasure. I drove to meet Julie, who is looking very well and is delighted to be with her family again.

December 3rd. On getting up this morning, I was much astonished to hear that Leopold and Julie had left at 4 o'clock for Münsterstadt (between Meiningen and Schweinfurt) where the Emperor Alexander had given them a "rendez-vous."

December 5th. Julie returned at 1 a.m. much pleased with the kind reception she had been accorded by the Emperor, but rather knocked up by this hurried little journey. Leopold has accompanied the Emperor to Weimar.

December 16th. With what pleasure I would have celebrated Leopold's birthday in his old home, were it not that he is so unhappy. I could not look at his dear face without a pang. This is already the 2nd birthday he spends without her, who was the joy and pride of his life. All felt depressed by his sorrow and the brightness usual on such an anniversary was therefore absent. I had a "déjeuner" for all, and in the evening there was a dinner at the Schloss, followed by a Tableau: "The return of a Pilgrim to his family," and then a rather tedious French comedy, the only point off which was that a part had been inserted and arranged for Louise who recited very prettily some specially written verses concerning her brother-in-law.

December 21st. To-day Louise has attained her 18th birthday. May God's blessing rest on her future! I went to her quite early and at 12 there was a "déjeuner" in my house. In the evening we all dined at the Schloss and attended a ball.

December 24th. In beautiful weather I lunched at Ketschendorf and went in the evening to Sophie for her Christmas tree and "Bescherung" for her children, which was most successful and they were very delighted with all their gifts. Julie, Leopold and everyone from the Schloss were also there. Christmas always reminds me of former happy days.

December 31st. In a few hours this year will have ended, already the third since I have lived in this house. The rapid flight of time quite dazes me but I am not much troubled by the thought that perhaps only a short part of my life remains. The happiest days of my life are long past and death will bring me release from my sorrows and troubles! Owing to so many painful experiences, my children have aged so prematurely in spirit, and I sometimes feel as if I were younger than they. If Sophie were in good health, I should be able to take more pleasure in the glowing youth of her dear boys. But her sufferings and melancholy frame of mind overcloud the evening of my life. But I will not end this year with complaints, as I have to thank God for so many joys and blessings, such as having Leopold and Julie with me. May my dear ones be preserved during the coming year and may I not have to weep over any fresh graves.

1819

January 2nd. May God's blessing rest on this day and on the whole of Ernest's life. May his fine, thriving little boy give him as much pleasure and be as good a son to him, as he has been to me. I gave Ernest a little "déjeuner" and took luncheon with him. There were a number of Bavarian officers at Court, who had come to pay their respects, on the occasion of his birthday. In the evening there was a ball opened by two quadrilles. The first represented the Seasons, in which Louise and Mensdorff took part as winter. The second quadrille represented peasants from the different Coburg districts. These peasant costumes always prove a great success.

January 19th. I cannot help closing this day with a certain amount of melancholy for to-day I have ended 62 years. I find old age creeping on imperceptibly, and cannot be thankful enough that as yet I notice so little this fact. I shall not mind any bodily ailments or discomforts, if only my mental powers preserve their youth. I had a delightful surprise whilst breakfasting with Julie at her house, who should walk in but Ferdinand. It was however a great disappointment that he came without Tony. I am truly grieved that she is not here too, and know how she must feel it. I find Ferdinand looking very thin, but in very good spirits. A very pretty little Comedy "Das Nachtlager von Granada," by Kind, was performed at the Schloss.

January 24th. We have celebrated Mensdorff's birthday rather sadly to-day. May God make this coming year happier for the good excellent man, who for the last year and a half has had a miserable time. His wife's sufferings and neurasthenic condition are a perpetual worry for him. They came late to a little "déjeuner" I had for them. Mensdorff, Hugo and Alphonse lunched at the Schloss, Sophie remaining at home, but in the evening I am glad to say, she got better, and even went to see her children act a little Play.

January 29th. For the first time in the new year, Ernest, Louise, Ferdinand, and Leopold, lunched with me at Ketschendorf. The weather was so fine that the whole party returned to town on foot.

February 4th. Ferdinand is leaving us again in two days. It has been a very short visit, only ten days, but still we have enjoyed it very much. I delighted in listening to his interesting conversations with Leopold, at breakfast time. The latter too will be leaving shortly. I dare not think of the breaking up of this pleasant companionship, or of the loneliness that will come over me when they are gone. One can, alas, no longer reckon on Sophie's society, since she has been so ill, and she is more or less lost to all her friends.

March 17th. I am going to-morrow with Leopold to Amorbach. He has been rather unwell lately and is still rather weak, so even this short journey frightens me. But I *must* see Victoire again, before she goes to England.

March 20th (Amorbach). Thank God, dear Victoire is looking very well and is thoroughly happy in her new married life! She undertakes the journey to England, which somewhat alarms me in her present condition, with joyful anticipation. After tea, we had some music and Feodore sang charmingly with her mother.

March 24th (Würzburg). Victoire is so overwhelmed with business, that I thought it better not to prolong my stay, so as not to be in the way. She starts on the 27th, making the journey by short day stages with her own horses as far as Brussels. Where she will spend a few days. The parting was very hard and Victoire was much upset. But I carried with me the comforting certainty that she is really happy and contented, and that Kent makes an excellent husband.

May 1st. I came early to Ketschendorf for I could no longer bear remaining alone in my house. I have not for a long time felt anything so much. For seven months I had Leopold living with me. We always breakfasted together, and in fact did most things together. It was so delightful having him with me and now everything seems so empty and dull!

May 4th. I can hardly write as I am feeling so depressed. I have just returned from Sophie. Everything was already packed up for to-morrow's departure. The children were running about mad with excitement at the prospect of the journey. Poor dear Sophie sat there weary and dispirited, dreading to-morrow's effort. Ernest was also there and finally Mensdorff came. I went home late with a very heavy heart.

May 5th. This morning at 10, they departed. Thank God, I have news of Victoire's safe arrival in England. I have just received a letter from the Duke of Kent, telling me that on the 23rd they crossed over in a high wind from Calais to Dover, taking four hours.

May 31st. The first thing I heard with great joy this morning was that an English courier had arrived with news of Victoire's safe delivery of a daughter.[1] I was so agitated by this information, that I could hardly get out a few words in English when speaking to Mr. Hill. I had been so anxious about that long journey, lest it might do her harm. God bless her and the precious child!

July 10th. A letter from Antoinette has decided me to start for Carlsbad where she will be arriving on the 17th or 18th. I am immensely looking forward to this meeting.

July 17th (Carlsbad). I am going to bed tired but very happy. At half-past three my brother and I drove as far as Engelhaus to meet Antoinette; it rained every few minutes and we had only just taken shelter in a shed, when she arrived in a "coupé" with Marie. At last I have seen her again, after ten long years. I cannot express my joy. Marie, who left us as a child, has shot up into a young lady, with a pretty slim figure, and a most attractive natural manner, improved by her life at a big Court. Antoinette has grown rather stout, but is looking as fresh and blooming as her nineteen-year-old daughter Marie. It is her sweet angelic nature, which has preserved her beauty. Bad temper so often spoils a once pretty face.

July 30th. We are having beautiful but intensely hot weather, and by the evening I am generally so tired, I can hardly write. The

[1] Later Queen Victoria of England, b. May 24, 1819, d. 1901.

running around to and from the springs, the afternoon calls, when one is so sleepy that it is an effort to make conversation, and the evening walk in the Promenade are all very exhausting, particularly as the hot nights allow one little rest.

August 3rd. There is a tremendous concourse of Diplomats here: Prince Metternich, Count Münster from Hannover, Richberg from Bavaria, and Ambassadors, Ministers and Statesmen of every kind. One can only hope that whatever they may be brewing, is for the happiness of Germany.

August 14th (Coburg). Thank goodness that I am back in my own pleasant home and surroundings! I was very thankful, at the last, to be leaving Carlsbad, as the heavy, damp air there did not suit me. I was here at 6, and Ernest and Louise arrived at the same time, she looking very well.

August 15th. I drove with Caroline to the Rosenau, where I found Fräulein Siebold[1] just returned from England and she could give me all the details about Victoire. I was longing for news and Fräulein Siebold gave me an excellent report of Victoire and of the little May flower.

August 18th. Antoinette is coming to-morrow and I can think of nothing else. It seems to me as if I could only thoroughly appreciate the joy of having her with me after ten years, in my own home. A mere meeting in a watering place is quite another thing.

August 19th. Worn out with fatigue and excitement, I end this day, which will always, even in after years, have the happiest of memories for me. Louise and I with her ladies, awaited Antoinette at Ketschendorf. Ernest had gone to Simau to meet her. At 5 o'clock she arrived, only accompanied by Marie and Buissy. We took tea at Ketschendorf. Antoinette was charmed with her little sister-in-law. After 6 we drove to the Rosenau and when we came into town, she

[1] Fräulein Charlotte von Siebold, the midwife who attended at the birth of Victoria, and subsequently at that of her future husband Albert three months later.

first got out a moment to visit Caroline, who was not quite well. Antoinette can hardly find her way about in the Schloss, it has been so much altered.

August 20th. Already at 8, I drove this morning to the Rosenau, and was just in time for breakfast. Antoinette afterwards took a walk with Ernest and I remained with Louise, who is not up to much exertion, as she is expecting a happy event very soon.

August 26th (Rosenau). I had no suspicion that Louise who was still so bright and well yesterday evening would be confined this morning, and went to be quite unconcernedly. At 7 a groom rode over bringing me the news that she had been safely delivered at 6 of a son.[1] Thank God, that the dreaded hour is now over and that a healthy little boy has been born. I hurried here, and found mother and child as well as possible, and Ernest overjoyed.

August 27th. It was a beautiful day and all is going well with dear Louise. The little boy is to be christened on the 29th, as I am leaving in a few days.

August 28th. When I came this afternoon to the Rosenau, I found that the plans for the Christening had been altered. The Duke of Gotha wishes to be present so it will now not take place for another 3 weeks. I am leaving for Prague on the 3rd and shall have to content myself with praying from a distance for the dear little boy, who is a very pretty child. Ernest wishes him to be given the old Saxon name of Albert.

September 1st. After tea, I took leave of Louise, who, with her little boy, is getting on very well.

September 6th. We drove away from Schlan this morning at 6, getting here at half-past ten. Sophie, overjoyed at my arrival, welcomed me at the foot of the stairs, and she was so excited, I feared it might do her harm. The dear boys rushed up to me with loud expressions of joy. All are much grown and look most flourishing. The morning passed by quickly sitting chatting with dear Sophie. In

[1] Prince Albert, later Prince Consort of England, d. 1861.

the afternoon we drove to meet Mensdorff, who came from Theresienstadt. I was so pleased to see the dear, excellent man again.

September 12th. What a delightful feeling it is to be able to go to rest now in Ferdinand's charming house. It seems to me like a dream, my being in Vienna, where I had never seriously thought of going. At 5 I left the little town of Znaim. The rod was very hilly and from every point one had lovely distant views. Already at Stockrau one approaches the beautiful wooded hills that spread out behind Vienna. I found Ferdinand awaiting me at Enzersdorf. We were mutually overjoyed at seeing each other, and he could hardly believe I had come all that way to pay him a visit. During the last hour of the drive, the scenery became indescribably lovely. We seemed to take ages driving through the never-ending town, for Ferdinand's house is in the outskirts right at the other end. I had expected Vienna to be a large town, but not so attractive. We reached Ferdinand's pretty house before 4. Tony, still looking so fresh and well, received me, quite trembling with excitement and pleasure. Antoinette, her husband, and children were also there. Ferdinand's fair-haired little boys are sweet children.

September 16th. It is really unfortunate that Ferdinand's duties keep him away the whole morning, so that much time is lost, in which we might have been together. When he returns, we sit in the garden. To-day we dined with Cohary[1] and the Württembergs.

October 6th (Walterskirchen).[2] I left Vienna with a heavy heart, having spent three such happy weeks there. I shall never forget all Ferdinand's touching care of me or Tony's evident pleasure at having me staying under their roof. Ferdinand started at 7 this morning and I, with Tony, and Malchen at 9. It is 5 stages on the Brünner road, and as soon as we came to the last stage, off the high road, the going became very bad, owing to the rain which had much spoilt the surface. We got here at 4, and at once had some food, after which, the weather being fine, we took a walk in the spacious garden, until the sun went down in its golden glory.

[1] Prince Joseph of Cohary, father of the Princess Antonia.
[2] Walterskirchen, property of the Prince of Cohary.

October 7th. To-day it rained unfortunately all day. Luckily the Schloss is a fine building and very comfortable. It forms a square, which surrounds the small courtyard. The sides of the building are surrounded by a beautiful large garden. The countryside is not pretty and very flat, but the soil is very fruitful. The rooms are lofty and light, not at all modern, but handsomely and comfortably furnished. After luncheon, we drove, in spite of the rain, to the huge Wine Cellars, containing a great provision of wine kept in colossally large vats. We spent a very pleasant evening all together.

October 9th (Znaim in Moravia). At 7 this morning I left Walterskirchen and its kind agreeable hosts, with much regret. The drive from Walterskirchen to Znaim goes along the Brünner road. Round Nickolsburg, a pretty little town, belonging to Prince Dietrichstein, the country is extremely attractive.

October 11th (Prague). It was very cold, and the moon still lit up the frosted trees, when I started this morning. The day became very fine. In Bohemia, the roads are much better and I got here at half-past seven. Hugo and Alphonse arrived directly after me, soon followed by Sophie and Mensdorff. I was thankful to find her looking fairly well, although she has been very ailing of late.

October 19th (Libkowitz). At 6 o'clock I drove away sadly, through the still dark streets of the ancient royal town. It was a dreary grey autumn day, the distance veiled in midst, and a drizzling rain soon setting in. It was completely dark by the time we got here at 8 o'clock.

October 22nd (Coburg). I got here in pouring rain, at 1 o'clock, having broken my journey at Eger and Culmbach. Louise had come into town, from Rodach, to receive me. Both she and Ernest, when he had returned from shooting, came to tea, afterwards going back to Rodach. I am glad to say that I found all my dear ones well.

October 25th (Rodach). I got here this afternoon in very dismal weather and could hardly repress my impatience to see the dear little boys again. Ernest is much grown and now runs about quite alone. Albert is a very pretty child, his blue eyes and small mouth reminding me of Antoinette at that age.

(The next months are missing).

1 8 2 0

January 2nd. This was once one of the brightest days of my life. May dear good Ernest be as happy a father as he has been a good son and may the noon and evening of his life be as serene as the morning. He too has had many troubles and anxieties but they have passed away like a thunderstorm, without seriously disturbing the happiness of his life. At 11 I gave a little déjeuner and also later a dinner.

January 19th. I began my birthday rather sadly. My first thoughts on awakening were for my dear absent ones and how I longed for the joy I had last year, when Leopold, Julie, Sophie, Mensdorff and the dear boys were all with me. My room seemed very empty when I went into it. But Ernest and Louise soon arrived with their little ones, my oldest friend Caroline also came, and what was quite a pleasant surprise my Ebersdorf nephew, whom his father had sent to convey his congratulations to me.

January 30th. A letter from Victoire dated the 17th rather worries me. Kent is seriously ill with pneumonia. He has already been bled twice, and Müller to whom I spoke has increased my anxiety.

(Another month missing.)

March 11th. The weather was so fine that I lunched at Ketschendorf. I need better air and more bright looking days, for I am suffering from constant headaches, and my nerves have not yet at all recovered from the painful shock of dear good Kent's death.[1]

[1] The Duke of Kent died on January 23, 1820, six days before his father, King George III.

March 20th. I went off to Ketschendorf on a fine bright morning, as I wanted to read in peace and quiet, a letter from Victoire, giving me all the details of her beloved husband's illness. Poor dear child, how my heart aches for her and how I am tormented by the haunting suspicion that the wretched doctors by their constant bleeding are responsible for the death of that splendid strong man. I could wring my hands in despair. Oh God, give me strength to bear this blow with resignation and calm!

April 25th. In a letter I have just got from Antoinette, she says she will be here the day after to-morrow. What a joy!

April 27th. Good Antoinette arrived this evening. I drove to meet her at Simau and brought her to her pleasant quarters, generally used by Sophie.

April 28th. I can hardly express my joy at having Antoinette at last again with me. Only now do I realise how lonely I have been feeling all this while, and how for many reasons I needed such a pleasant diversion. Antoinette with her children and suite took their meals with me here, and we went to Ketschendorf for tea.

May 9th. Württemberg has arrived with his two A.D.C.s.

May 16th. My brother and sister-in-law arrived this evening, and we received them at Ketschendorf, driving later into town. They are staying with me.

May 21st. To-day is a typical Whitsunday. Flowers out everywhere, and people walking about enjoying themselves. In the afternoon, I took a drive with my brother and Harry.

May 23rd (Ketschendorf). At last I have been able to move in here. Much against my will, I have missed most of the beautiful May days but I find it very difficult now always to carry out what I want.

July 11th (Würzburg). At 4 this morning I left Coburg. It was a glorious day and the country looked indescribably beautiful in the bright sunshine, all the luxurious vegetation was unusually green after the late refreshing rains. The roads were good and I got here at half-past eight.

July 12th (Heidelberg). I have had a longer day's journey than I expected. Weather and road were splendid. Part of the way was very bleak and uninteresting. Only near Mosbach, after which we entered the picturesque valley of the Neckar, did it become really pretty, but unfortunately twilight had already set in.

July 13th (Baden-Baden). I drove away from Heidelberg on a lovely morning. The beauty of the scenery in all its summer glory is impossible to describe. But unfortunately before getting here it started to rain. Dear Julie welcomed me with such joy!

July 14th. Julie, Antoinette and I live in one house together, and could dispense with all other society, of which there does not seem to be very much at present, excepting the Royal Families of Bavaria and Baden. With the kind thoughtfulness to them the King[1] and Queen[2] of Bavaria and Princess Amelie of Baden came immediately to see us this afternoon. I was particularly glad to meet the King[1] again. He is an old friend of my youth, and I had not seen him for 30 years. Afterwards we drove to the Convent Lichtenthal, and on beyond, through valleys richly wooded with walnut and chestnut trees.

July 16th. It was very fine and warm to-day, and I drank the waters amidst the pretty surroundings. The rich vegetation of this country makes every place most attractive. In the afternoon Antoinette, Marie, and I visited the Dowager Grand Duchess at the Schloss. The road is steep, and passes an old and lonely Schloss, where Stephanie lives and rules, like a Princess in a fairy tale. She is no longer as pretty as when I saw her ten years ago, but she is much more friendly and has really become a very pleasant little woman. The Schloss is very big and the dungeons still show signs of having been used by the infamous "Vehmgericht."

[1] Maximilian Joseph, King of Bavaria, reigned 1806-25.
[2] Queen Caroline, b. Princess of Baden.

July 27th. Directly after luncheon, I drove with Julie and Malchen to the ruins of the old ancestral home of the Baden family. In the midst of the forest stands what remains of this ancient Castle, overlooking a large stretch of country. Nothing could be more picturesque than the gateways, amidst the gloom of the forest, when the sun strikes the ancient walls. Trees and bushes grow amongst the ruins. A little above the Castle, on a great rock, stands a tower at the foot of which is the so-called "Rittersaal." The view over the vast Rhine valley, with the beautiful forest in the foreground, is unique. These lovely remnants of vanished greatness have a peculiar attraction. The old tower is very imposing, and the lower part of it may possibly date as far back as the Romans.

July 28th. In heavenly weather we all drove out into the valley of the Murg, and then along the river to the Castle of Eberstein. This beautiful ancient building was somewhat clumsily restored by the Margrave Frederick, brother of the present Grand Duke. The old gate is still standing and in the corner of the courtyard there is an ancient well. Small towers and a vaulted Hall are still survivals of olden times. We also visited the "Favorite," a small country residence in the neighbourhood of Rastatt, which is most interesting. It was built at the commencement of the last century by the Margravine Sybylla Augusta, a Princess of Saxe-Lauenstein, and it is still furnished exactly as she left it. The rooms are beautiful and the evening sun streaming in at the windows lit up the empty building, in which that vain and beautiful woman held sway. In one room she is portrayed seventy times in different costumes! The full moon was already high in the sky by the time we got back to Baden.

July 30th. This morning I carried out my wish, to see the ruins of the Ebersteinberg, the oldest in the country. I drove with my lady as far as the village of Eberstein and from there walked up to the ruins. It was very hot and the road was very steep, and I don't remember having ever been so hot in my life as I was by the time I reached the old dark eyrie which hangs on the edge of a rock. From there one overlooks the wide through which the Rhine winds its way, and in the distance the Vosges mountains. We returned to the village, and the walk down over loose stones was even more exhausting than the ascent. We drove through the Forest, to the old Castle, the views were marvellous, but the Castle did not look quite so picturesque as it did in the evening light.

July 31st (Heidelberg). I left Baden this morning, and parted with a heavy heart from dear Julie, who accompanied me as far as the "Favorite." We sat in the garden of the little Palace. The few pleasant weeks spent at Baden with my daughters passed all too quickly. Julie has promised me that I shall see her next year at Coburg, but a long dreary winter lies between me and this promised visit. Occupied with these sad thoughts, we drove on to Bruchsal, where we broke the journey for a short hour. As we were passing through the Bergstrasse, the sun was just setting behind the hills. We got here at 9, and found in the Hotel most comfortable and cool rooms.

August 3rd (Coburg). We arrived here this afternoon in glorious weather. No one is here, excepting Caroline. Everyone else is in Rodach. I took tea with her in Mensdorff's garden.

August 4th. Ernest, Louise, and their little boys came this morning into town to see me. I found the children much grown. We lunched in the "Herrngarten," and we all spent the evening here.

August 7th. Ernest came for a moment early this morning, to tell me that the Duke of Gotha had announced his arrival for to-morrow morning at 4! This lack of consideration is typical.

September 17th. Marie has spent her 21st birthday here, at Ketschendorf, where I am now staying. May God's blessing accompany the dear sweet girl through life! I have many hopes for her, though I do not dare to formulate them. Painful experience has taught me that our wishes are perhaps not always wise in God's eyes. I started early for town and went at once to Antoinette. There was a big "déjeuner" in Mensdorff's garden, and the weather was so fine that we dined in the Herrngarten. Now, at 11 o'clock, I have returned to Ketschendorf in the most beautiful moonshine where a little ball in Marie's honour finished off the day.

September 19th. At half-past six this morning I drove off alone with my maid, in my new English carriage, the first comfortable one I have ever possessed.

September 20th (Carlsbad). I started a little too late and only got here at 9 o'clock, this evening.

September 21st (Schlan). The whole day was dreary and the scenery from Carlsbad here, at all times unattractive, looked hopelessly grim. The Autumn is further advanced here, than with us, owing to the long drought, and most of the trees are either yellow, or have lost most of their leaves. Towards 8, we reached this quiet clean little inn.

September 22nd. At 7, in beautiful sunshine, we left Schlan. A little before getting to Prague, Sophie, with Hugo, Alphonse and Alexander, came to meet me. I do not find her altered in appearance or manner and she walks quite well in the rooms and even up and downstairs. The boys and much grown. We were delighted to see one another again. Mensdorff is unfortunately still with his Brigade.

September 23rd. I have just returned from the theatre, not so much impressed with the performance, which was poor, as with the glorious moonlight, which lit up all the large buildings and the high old towers and gateways of the city.

September 24th. We drove this afternoon up the Hradschin, and walked in the Palace gardens, where I had never been before. They are spacious and shady and full of fruit trees and rare plants. At the end, from the bastion one has a splendid view over the town, the river, and the distant hills.

September 27th. We were just going out for a drive, when a carriage drove up, and Mensdorff, whom we had only expected to-morrow, stepped out. I was delighted to see him again, and found him looking very well.

September 28th. Before going to the play, we drove to the "Rossmarkt." It being the Feast of St. Wenzel, Bohemia's first Christian ruler and Patron Saint. Is statue was decorated with flowers, altars were being erected in his honour, and the Square was lit up with small lanterns and there were candles at every window. A large number of the inhabitants were walking about quietly and decorously. In front of the altars people were praying and singing. It was a beautiful sight in the calm warm night and I would have gladly remained longer.

October 1st. Today was a real summer's day. I drove this morning with Sophie to the "Lorenzo-Berg" where many old walls are still to be seen, the ruins of a fortress built by Charles IV. We seated ourselves in front of the Lorenzo Chapel, from which one has a very extensive view, and then went further down the hill to the Hasenburg where the view was still finer, though not so extensive. In the afternoon we drove to Bubnitsch, where Sophie remined sitting with her boys, whilst I took a walk with Mensdorff. The evening sun was already setting behind the trees, its last golden rays lighting up the whole countryside. I wandered with Mensdorff through the spacious Park which in many parts is most beautiful.

October 6th. To-morrow I must leave my dear ones, and I dare not dwell on it. I have been so happy here, and should have been even more so had it not been for an odious catarrh which has been tormenting me, almost since the beginning of my stay, making me often feel quite ill.

October 7th (Schlan). Here I am sitting again, sad and lonely, where only a fortnight ago I had been awaiting with joyous anticipation the coming day. 'Voilà la vie." The parting with Sophie, her husband and boys, was very painful to me. I lunched in Prague before starting and they all accompanied me as far as the "Weissen Berg."

October 9th (Coburg). Everything here is still looking extra-ordinarily green and summery. In Bohemia it was already like November, whereas here, it is like September and it is very pleasant to see leaves on the tree. Ernest, Louise and Antoinette came from the Rosenau to see me, also Württemberg and Caroline.

October 13th. It freezes every night and the cold sharp air, which no sun seems to be able to warm, makes my cough very troublesome.

November 5th. To-day has been really fine, and I drove with Antoinette to Rodach to pay my first visit to the family there, and returned after 5.

December 9th. I have been very ailing for some days past. My cough has become worse again and I have such difficulty in breathing, than often in the nights I feel as if I were choking.

December 10th (Sunday). For days I have not been able to leave the house. To-day I had wanted to go to the Schloss, but I was too knocked up, by a sleepless night and suffocating spasms.

December 14th. The weather is clearer and brighter and I am in consequence feeling better and breathing more freely.

December 17th. The cold during this week has made me worse again. The few brighter days did not last long. The state of my health this winter reminds me painfully that the last stage of my life is no longer far off. Winter is always a bad time for me, but never have I experienced before to such an extent the weakness of old age. My days are in Thy hands, oh Heavenly Father, and Thou hast numbered them. In calm faith I Thy goodness, I continue on my way.

December 24th. Christmas Eve always makes me rather melancholy, as it recalls vanished happy days. I went to Antoinette and saw her beautiful Christmas tree and all the presents. Louise and the children had theirs at the Schloss. I was tired and not feeling very well, by the time I got back.

December 31st. I close this year ill and depressed, and I look forward rather sadly to the future. Merciful God, Thou hast aided me in the past and Thy hand will surely be stretched out now, to help me when I need it most! I have no wish beyond the hope, that when the end comes, it will be peaceful. This year has brought me many pleasures but also one great sorrow. Already since last January my dear son-in-law Kent rests in his grave, he who was so happy and made others happy. In the year that is about to begin may I be protected in every trial that may come to me. I feel certain that all will be for the best.

1821

January 2nd. May God bless this year for Ernest and give him wisdom and power to act aright. I have just returned very weary from the Schloss, where Ernest's birthday was celebrated by a ball, which my tired brain is incapable of describing.

January 16th. My brother, his wife and Linette[1] are coming for my birthday, but I am afraid I shall have to receive them in bed, as I am feeling so ill.

February 10th. I had to take to my bed on the 17th of January, and the following day my guests arrived, rather to my dismay, for I had a good deal of fever and was feeling rather bad, so that leeches and God knows what other remedy had to be employed, and finally the pain lessened. I have been up again for a week, but still feel very shaky and am sleeping badly and not eating. Since my youth, no illness has pulled me down so much, and I fear the trouble is not over.

May 24th. At last, after 14 weeks, I am able to write a few words, but not without exhaustion. I have been very near death, but God in His mercy has spared me, for which I am deeply thankful.

May 29th. I have once more had the pleasure of my sister spending her birthday quietly with me. We lunched with the Württembergs, and good Antoinette arranged a cheerful little "goûter" in the garden of Simau. We remained there, till the cool of the evening drove me away.

June 19th. For the first time since my illness I heard some music yesterday. I wished so much to hear the choruses out of "La Gazza

[1] Caroline, Princess of Reuss-Ebersdorf.

Ladra." They were sung in my drawing-room. Though I enjoyed it very much, it rather tired me.

June 25th. Yesterday morning, the Duchess of Gotha, who arrived a week ago at the Rosenau, came to see me, and I was very exhausted by her prolonged visit.

June 28th. It is much quieter here now, as Ferdinand and Tony have moved on to the Rosenau, and I find that a calmer atmosphere is good for me, as I can no longer stand much movement around me. Nothing fatigues me more than much talking. Ferdinand and his dear wife come often to see and take a meal with me, and on fine days I go to the Rosenau, but not too often, as the Duchess of Gotha's extreme deafness, and the shouting that it entails, are a perfect torture to me.

July 7th (Ketschendorf). I came here on a beautiful morning, to try to complete my recovery undisturbed. I am able to write very little as yet, and never of an evening. In the afternoon my sister comes to me.

September 22nd (Lobenstein). I left here at 5 in the morning. The road as far as Cronach was passable, and the weather splendid. The Main at Lichtenfels is as broad as the Rhine, and there was much activity on the river, and on its banks. The road from Cronach here was, in consequence of the endless rain, deep in slush. I got here at 6, having broken my journey for luncheon at Steinwiesen. My sister Fanny drove as far as Hornsgrun, to meet me.

September 27th. To-day it was the birthday of my eldest Ebersdorf niece, and we drove over to breakfast with them and brought dear Linette our little gifts. Then we went with my brother to Heirichstein. After luncheon he drove me through the village and through its outskirts, old and new, where I recognised many a favourite haunt of my youth. It is extraordinary how insignificant places appear to one in later years, which in one's youth seemed so important. Only the plantation I remember seeing laid out by my good Father does not appear to have shrunk, on the contrary, it has grown and improved with the years.

September 29th. In a fearful storm, which made one think the world was coming to an end, we lunched at Belle Vue, and as the roads dry very quickly in these parts, we were later able to go for a walk.

October 1st. I must somehow have caught a chill on my drive back from Ebersdorf yesterday, and feel very unwell. I have such pains in my limbs, that I am afraid I must be feverish.

October 3rd. I had such pains in my head and palpitations of the heart this morning that I could not help being alarmed about myself, but it passed off, and we were able to lunch in the little Casino at the foot of the old tower, the Ebersdorf family joining us.

(The Diary ends here.)

Augusta, Dowager Duchess of Saxe-Coburg-Saalfeld, died in Coburg on November 16, 1831, aged 74

Other reprints available in this series

All titles include a new introduction or foreword written specially for
and unique to these editions

Russia

Life of Alexander II, F.E. Grahame
Alexander III, Tsar of Russia, Charles Lowe
The Emperor Nicholas II as I knew him, Sir John Hanbury-Williams
At the Court of the last Tsar, A.A. Mossolov
The Intimate Life of the Last Tsarina, Princess Catherine Radziwill
My mission to Russia and other Diplomatic Memories, Sir George
    Buchanan
The reign of Rasputin: An Empire's Collapse, M.V. Rodzianko
*Collected Works: Once a Grand Duke, Always a Grand Duke, Twilight of
    Royalty*, Alexander, Grand Duke of Russia
Memories of Russia 1916-1919, Princess Paley

Germany

Frederick, Crown Prince and Emperor, Rennell Rodd
Letters of the Empress Frederick, edited by Sir Frederick Ponsonby
*Between two Emperors: The Willy-Nicky Telegrams and Letters, 1894-
    1914*
My Memoirs, Princess Victoria of Prussia
Potsdam Princes, Ethel Howard
Seven Years at the Prussian Court, Edith Keen
My Own Story, Louisa of Tuscany, Ex-Crown Princess of Saxony **and**
    Memoirs of the Husband of an Ex-Crown Princess, Enrico Toselli (in one
    volume)

England

Richard III, Sir Clements Markham
The Witchery of Jane Shore, C.J.S. Thompson
His Royal Highness The Duke of Connaught and Strathearn, Sir George
  Aston
Sidelights on Queen Victoria, Sir Frederick Ponsonby

Austria

Emperor Francis Joseph of Austria, Joseph Redlich
My Past: Reminiscences of the Courts of Austria and Bavaria, Marie
  Larisch
Recollections of a Royal Governess [governess to Archduchess Elizabeth],
  Anon.

Roumania

The Story of my Life (Vols. I-III in one volume), Marie, Queen of
  Roumania

Serbia

*A Royal Tragedy: Being the Story of the Assassination of King Alexander
  and Queen Draga of Servia,* Chedomille Mijatovich

Miscellaneous

*The Complete Works: The Journal of a Disappointed Man, A Last Diary,
  Enjoying Life and other Literary Remains,* W.N.P. Barbellion

For further details please see *amazon.co.uk/amazon.com*

More titles are in preparation

Printed in Great Britain
by Amazon